COMMUNITY OF GRACE

AN ORTHODOX
CHRISTIAN YEAR
IN ALASKA

Mary Alice Cook

Conciliar Press • Chesterton, Indiana

Community of Grace
An Orthodox Christian Year in Alaska

Published by   Conciliar Press
                  A division of Conciliar Media Ministries
                  P.O. Box 748
                  Chesterton, IN 46304

Printed in the United States of America

ISBN 10: 1-936270-07-2

ISBN 13: 978-1-936270-07-1

    15 14 13 12 11 10   6 5 4 3 2 1

For Barbara

CONTENTS

AUTHOR'S NOTE

IT HAS BEEN MORE THAN TEN YEARS SINCE BARBARA DUNAWAY first suggested that I write what she called "a history of the St. John's church and community." I *wanted* to write it, but I couldn't figure out *how* to write it. Once God showed me that the only way to tell the story of my home was through the stories of the people who make it my home, everything fell into place.

There is not space enough here to mention everyone who contributed to the writing of this book, because *everyone* contributed. To my St. John's community: I love you and thank you.

FOREWORD

THIRTY-FIVE YEARS AGO A "CALL FOR COMMUNITY" WAS PART of the essential beginnings of our church in Eagle River, Alaska. What we meant by that "call," we said, was to make the church a priority in your life and to live near the church, ideally within walking distance. In this way we hoped to give practical expression to the Christian call for love, forgiveness, accountability, and care for one another. We were also fortunate that our neck of the woods was being developed at the same time our church was growing. This allowed people to buy land near the church and to build their own homes.

We recognized at that time, in the 1970s, that normal, human community, which had existed for thousands of years as the take-it-for-granted fabric of human life, was all of a sudden in our modern world in danger of disintegrating. This was caused mostly by the extreme mobility of our society brought on by the airplane and the automobile. So, we posited, why can't the Church itself address this problem directly and be for Christians a vehicle by which people are called back to normal human life, back to community?

It seemed like a simple idea at the time, but the astonishing thing is that it worked. As our church grew it did become an intentional, geographically close community, so that today, around Saint John Cathedral located on Monastery Drive in Eagle River, over fifty families who are members live within a mile. And now that community is

7

also made up of members who are part of a second and third generation. The looming question before us presently is, can the experiment
continue?

In this book Mary Alice Cook is not writing a history of Saint
John's. What she wanted to do was to write about "intentional community." And she accomplished this, I think, in a brilliant way. She tells
the stories of a few people's lives and weaves them together around the
liturgical life of the Church as it moves through the cycle of the year.
This experience of liturgical life is certainly nothing we Bible-study-
only evangelicals would have expected thirty-five years ago. But now
for our community it is at the heart of everything. The rhythm of Lent
and Easter, flowing into Pentecost, followed by other fasting seasons
and feast days and then leading up to Christmas and Epiphany, all the
while interspersed with baptisms and weddings and funerals, is the
real fabric of our community. And this is certainly not anything we
could have ever figured out on our own. Not by a long stretch. Rather
it was the gift of the Orthodox Church, where God in His mercy and
providence brought us eventually to land.

One last thing I would add in looking back over the years is that
such a church community has to exist in the tension of two vital things:
commitment and freedom. Commitment is necessary to build anything valuable in this life, especially something that is so contrary to
the flow of the modern world. Commitment to community means not
automatically relocating when conflicts arise or you tire of the weather
or you get a better job offer in another state. It means choosing to stay
put and to struggle alongside lifelong friends. But the other essential
thing for a healthy community is freedom. That means freedom for
people to move away, for children to leave as they grow up, for them
even to reject the Faith in which they were raised, and yet at the same

time to still be loved and respected in their choice. It also means a genuine openness to allow new people to fit in easily and become a part.
The center of any church and therefore of any "church community"
has to be Jesus Christ and His message about the Kingdom of God.
But Christ's call for all to follow Him and to seek the narrow way was
always given in the context of freedom, and so it must still be today.

As I said above, Mary Alice did not intend to write a history of
Saint John's. What she has done instead is to pull out of the fabric of
our community a handful of strands and tell the stories of a few particular people. The stories she has chosen to tell are no more special than
anyone else's. They are just the stories she knew best and the ones she
wanted to gather in order, once again, to make a "call for community."

> FR. MARC DUNAWAY
> St. John's Cathedral
> April 13, 2010

INTRODUCTION

A PLACE WITH PURPOSE

Therefore, let him who until now has had the privilege of living a common Christian life with other Christians praise God's grace from the bottom of his heart. Let him thank God on his knees and declare: It is grace, nothing but grace, that we are allowed to live in Christian community with Christian brethren.
— DIETRICH BONHOEFFER

IT IS A FRIGID FEBRUARY AFTERNOON, AND THE HOUSES along Monastery Drive—the street where I live—hunker quietly in the cold, clouds of vapor rising from them like household incense. Even though the daylight hours are beginning to stretch noticeably, tantalizing us with thoughts of spring, the pale Alaskan sun still hangs low on the horizon before fading early. Then, for a long night, the houses will be enclosed in frozen, starry darkness.

Outside one of the houses, I stand in a silent, waiting crowd. We watch as the door opens and several men, clothed in flowing black robes, walk out. They carry a cross, a smoking censer, and a large banner of a resolute Christ who appears to be standing atop an open grave. Other men follow, struggling through the doorway with a wooden coffin, plain except for a carving of an unusually shaped cross. The coffin is placed inside a waiting station wagon. A procession forms, the robed men leading, the car slowly following, my neighbors and I bringing up the rear, singing a song in a minor key. We make our way down Monastery, an unspooling ribbon of shiny ice that leads to a church and, a little farther on, to a small cemetery.

At the church, the coffin is carried into the nave and set in place before the altar and the great icon of the Ascension, in which Christ is surrounded by angels as His apostles and Mary, His mother, watch from below. The coffin lid is removed, and we begin to chant the prayers that will continue throughout the long, candlelit night.

A watcher who is familiar with Alaska history—who knows that Alaska was first visited by Russian Orthodox monks in 1794, and that it is home to a large number of Russian Orthodox believers, a great many of them Alaska Natives who live in places first touched by those early missionaries—would recognize these bearded men in cassocks as Orthodox priests, and the carved cross as the Russian one with its third tilted crosspiece. The watcher might assume that this procession is happening in a small Alaska Native village, somewhere in the vast Alaskan Bush.

That assumption would be wrong.

We are not Alaska Natives, the spiritual descendants of the first Russian Orthodox believers. Most of us are white Americans, many of Protestant or Catholic background, converts to the Orthodox Church. We do not live in a remote Alaskan village, but in Eagle River, a bedroom community on the northern edge of Anchorage's urban sprawl. Our Orthodox heritage is rooted in Damascus, not Moscow.

We are the community of the Cathedral of St. John the Evangelist, and the procession we make on this wintry afternoon is part of the Orthodox ritual of burying the dead. It appears foreign to modern American eyes, and it is just one of many changes, great and small, that we have experienced in our understanding of theology, in the way we worship, and in the way we live with each other.

When "Grammy" Phyllis was laid to rest that day in 1992, I, along with my husband and our three children, watched the unfamiliar ritual through the eyes of the newly illumined. We had been *chrismated* (the service of anointing that seals one's reception into the Church) just one week earlier. The five of us had converted—literally, *turned*—from the busy superhighway of American Protestantism onto the less-traveled road of Orthodoxy. I recall attending this funeral, not because of my attachment to Grammy Phyl—I had never met her—but because I sensed, without being told, that the entire St. John's community would be present that day, and I longed to be one of them. It was this same desire for community that led our family to sell the Anchorage house we had loved for fourteen years to move to our own place on Monastery Drive.

The roots of the church and community of St. John's go back to 1968, when a man named Harold Dunaway was sent by Campus Crusade for Christ (a para-church Christian organization on college campuses and military bases) to evangelize the soldiers stationed in Anchorage. He was good at his job, and his wife Barbara had a tender heart and a soft shoulder. They soon found themselves surrounded by a group of lonely young soldiers and their friends, who crowded into the Dunaways' small apartment to talk about God and grace and forgiveness.

Campus Crusade did not have a plan for what to do with its

new converts, and Harold was reluctant to send them to the local churches. That, he thought, would be like "putting new wine into old wineskins." Most of the organized churches in Anchorage, he believed, were mired in tradition and legalism.

Harold decided that what he really wanted was to find a place where he could get away with a small group of young people, where they could study together and learn God's will for their lives. So he resigned from Campus Crusade, formed his own ministry, and purchased a big house on five acres at the end of a gravel road in Eagle River.

In 1972, when Barbara Dunaway moved into the big house, it looked like a derelict ship adrift in a sea of rocks and weeds. But she had a vision, one that was inspired by Edith Schaeffer's story of L'Abri, the community in Switzerland that she founded with her husband, Francis, the well-known Christian pastor and theologian. In her book, *L'Abri,* Mrs. Schaeffer described the pastoral beauty of her home, the daily routine of chores, meal preparation, and study, and the many guests who sought them out and were welcomed with food, a place to sleep, and, best of all, meaningful conversation.

Right away, Barbara picked out a cozy, wood-paneled room in the big house and named it the Library/Guest Room. Even then, she knew it would be important to have a place ready for the many guests who would come their way. Then she and Harold, their children, and the nine young people who had joined them set about transforming the neglected house and grounds into what she envisioned, a "place with purpose."

Don and Talitha, a young Army couple, moved into a trailer next door and went up to the main house for dinner every night. Their two-year-old daughter called it "the Big House," and the name stuck. The people in the Big House worshipped informally on Saturday nights. Sitting on beanbag cushions on the living room floor, they strummed guitars and sang Jesus songs. They were young and zealous, and one of their early group activities was leafleting Anchorage parking lots with information about the failure of the organized churches.

During those early years, Harold started each day with his Bible, a cigarette, and an ashtray, seated in front of a big window. Looking out at the northern horizon, at the white peaks of Mt. McKinley shimmering in the distance, he asked God to tell him what to do next. He could never have predicted what the answer would be.

In the mid-1970s, a providential chain of circumstances reconnected Harold with some of his colleagues from the old Campus Crusade days. He learned that many of them had, like himself, become disaffected with the organization and resigned. Some had formed their own "house churches," similar to what he was doing in Alaska.

What's more, seven of his old friends had banded together and were engaged in what they kiddingly called "the phantom search for the perfect church," or, more seriously, the effort to answer the question: Where and what is the Church of the New Testament? Harold trusted his friends and kept in close touch with them, and it soon became apparent that the answer to his own prayer about what to do with his group in Eagle River was being answered through that band of seven men.

Gradually, the Eagle River community moved away from informal praise worship to services that were more organized and traditional. Saturday evening worship in the Big House living room became a Sunday morning meeting on the second floor of another building. The community gathered in this "Upper Room" for a service roughly patterned on the ancient liturgy of the Eastern Orthodox Church. After prayers, hymns, and a sermon, the people separated into six groups and went to six different homes for their communion service. They called themselves Grace Community Church.

Eventually, Harold and his people in Eagle River joined those original seven searchers and a confederation of congregations in an organization they named the New Covenant Apostolic Order. Later, the confederation changed its name to the Evangelical Orthodox Church. In April 1987, having finally been let in on "the best-kept secret in America," these congregations, including the group at the newly named St. John the Evangelist Orthodox Cathedral in Eagle River, were received *en masse* by His Eminence, Metropolitan (Archbishop) PHILIP Saliba, into the canonical Antiochian Orthodox Christian Archdiocese of North America.[1]

During those years of changing and learning, people got married, had children, and bought land near the church. For a few years, it seemed that almost every weekend neighbors got together for another "house raising." Many families built homes that included extra rooms for boarders and guests or apartments for singles or a small family. Some pooled their money to build side-by-side duplexes. They were forming an "intentional community," a group of people who came together deliberately in a residential setting, united around a specific vision and shared values.

There was never a "master plan" to create a community around the Cathedral. People simply wanted to live near each other. Neither has there ever been a blueprint for how to grow the membership. What

---

1   A complete story of the Evangelical Orthodox can be found in *Becoming Orthodox* by Fr. Peter Gillquist, published by Conciliar Press.

brings people here is folks inviting friends and family to come and see what it is all about. And people keep coming.

Today, in a small valley near the slopes of the Chugach Mountains, the community that was born in the Big House and is growing up in the Cathedral includes many more houses, a school, two parish houses, a chapel, and a cemetery. Several dozen families live within walking distance of the Cathedral, and others who want to live here are waiting for housing or land to become available. A number of families live elsewhere in Eagle River and in Anchorage. Whenever I use the word *community*, I am referring to *everyone* who has joined his or her life with the faithful at St. John's.

We get many curious visitors, especially during our short Alaskan summer. They drive their rented cars and RVs slowly up Monastery Drive, between plain, wooden houses, and catch sight of the schoolhouse, the little cemetery, and beyond it the golden domes of St. Sergius Chapel, glinting among the birches. They turn in at the copper-domed Cathedral, they admire the lawn drawn up to it like a warm green blanket with flowers and children scattered on top, and they ask: "What is this place? Who are these people? Why are they here and what are they doing?"

This book is an effort to answer those questions. It is a scrapbook of memories and stories, observations and reflections, gleaned from my seventeen years of living here, all of it bound together within the Orthodox Church year of feasts and fasts.

We Orthodox Christians in Eagle River are not separatists, and we do not live together communally. Our little community is not a religious utopia—a Greek word, by the way, that means *nowhere*. We simply live, quite intentionally, in a neighborhood that gives us plenty of opportunity to put into practice the ideal of loving one another—

and learning what it means to bear one another's burdens—not just on Sunday, but all week long.

> *The word "community" usually refers to a way of being together that gives us a sense of belonging.*
>
> —HENRI NOUWEN

FALLING DOMINOES

FEBRUARY

FEAST OF THE PRESENTATION OF THE LORD

Rejoice, O Mother of God, Virgin full of grace; for from you has arisen the Sun of Righteousness, Christ our God, who gives light to those in darkness. Do you also, O righteous Elder, be glad of heart, who receive in your arms the Christ who has set free our souls and has bestowed upon us resurrection. —TROPARION (HYMN) OF THE FEAST

ON A CHILLY, DAMP EVENING LAST SUMMER, I WALKED THE half-mile or so from my house up Monastery Drive to the Cathedral. The bells tolled nine o'clock, and I looked up at the cupola just as the clouds parted, allowing rays of sunlight to strike the north side of the church. I watched the cedar wall begin to glow, like one of those "paintings of light" that bewitch the eye with their blend of color and shade. Then the wall seemed to catch fire and blaze and I stared, transfixed, until the sun moved and the light faded, leaving me with a feeling of helpless gratitude that I live on this beautiful road in this awesome state.

And then there are other times, like today, when the snow is piled six feet deep on either side of the driveway and winter is only half over and the sun will not show itself over the mountains until after noon, and that's only if it is clear and not overcast, which it often isn't. Christmas, the Super Bowl, and my New Year's resolutions are all over and done with. My SAD lamp (a remedy for Seasonal Affective Disorder, the "winter blues") is giving me a headache, and I feel very sorry that I ever had to even hear about Alaska, much less live here.

My relationship with my adopted state is like that—frequently satisfying, sometimes disappointing, and, on rare occasions, sublime. I'm only guessing, but I suspect that I speak for more people who live here than do those who get down on their knees every day and thank God that, of all the places on earth, He saw fit to put them here. Not everybody's picture is that black and white.

In spite of the midwinter gloom, the Church has put a celebration on the calendar for today. It is the Feast of the Presentation of the Lord in the Temple, the day the infant Jesus was first brought by Mary and Joseph into the Temple in Jerusalem. Unlike Christmas and Easter and Pentecost, this is one of those feasts that my Southern Baptist family never heard of, an event not much mentioned in our collective decades of Sunday School and Vacation Bible School classes.

My family—husband Bill and sons Adam, Justin, and Travis—jumped from the Baptist ship twenty years ago because of disturbing changes in its worship and ordinances. The midsized church we attended launched a campaign to grow its membership and, as part of that effort, decided to become more in tune with the culture and its changing tastes. A small music combo debuted in the worship service, and the vocal solos were usually of the closed-eyes, yearning female variety. The good old hymns were replaced by repetitive "praise choruses" that seemed intended to induce swaying, hand-raising, and a trancelike state, all novelties in an otherwise no-nonsense Southern Baptist service. Bill and I took to calling it a religious floor show.

But a far more serious concern was the proliferation of rebaptisms. Now, the climax of the Baptist worship service has always been the singing of the "invitation hymn" with its exhortation to come forward and be saved. It seemed that every Sunday we watched as some poor soul, agonizing over whether she was *really* saved or only *thought* she was saved, came forward and asked the preacher to rebaptize her so she could make sure. Our breaking point came when a ten-year-old child went forward at the invitation and requested his third baptism. The beaming preacher told the congregation that this child would certainly be baptized again. "After all," he said with a smile, "the third time's the charm!"

Whether the preacher's willingness to perform multiple baptisms on the same person had anything to do with growing the church membership, I can't say. But we found the practice appalling, and I think the day that confused child found his "charm" was the day we decided that the Baptists—at least the ones we knew about—were seriously off course.

But we did not jump ship right then and there, because there were no waiting arms to jump into. It would be a few more years before we would hear, by the purest chance, about the Orthodox Church and the community of St. John's in Eagle River. Like many an event that turns lives upside down, our conversion did not happen in a blinding second of revelation, but instead dawned gradually as we read, talked, questioned, and, most of all, simply stood in the Liturgy and listened.

Sometimes Bill and I say, "We must have passed Monastery Drive a thousand times since we moved to Anchorage thirty-four years ago. Why couldn't we have heard about this community back then? It would have saved us so much trouble." In the logical half of my brain, I know that is nonsense. Reactionary as we were, we'd have scorned those religious free spirits who lived here then, with their long hair and bushy beards and their mistrust of the organized churches. No, if we had been invited to join the happy group at the Big House, we might have visited once or twice, but I don't believe we would have stuck.

This is the pure chance that brought us to St. John's: A friend attended a college class with a woman who lived in the community. She invited him to visit, so he did, and then suggested to us that we do the same. He wasn't church shopping, and there was no reason for him to believe that we were either; he just thought it was an interesting scene. And as with so many of our neighbors, our "pure chance" turned out to be an amazing blessing.

So here we are, grateful to be here and grateful for the faithfulness of our Christian parents, who saw to it that a firm foundation was laid in our lives, preparing us for the home we found for ourselves and our children in the Orthodox Church. Our house on Monastery Drive (the street is named for a convent of nuns who lived here years ago, whose story I will tell later) is, as my friend Laura once said, "within the sound of the bells," and on this Sunday morning they are ringing, calling us to Divine Liturgy, the main service in Orthodox worship.

We walk carefully on the hard polished surface of Monastery Drive, mindful of the mirrorlike ice. Winter has swagged our neighbors' decks and fence rails with festive, puffy ribbons of white. In the thick trees on either side of Monastery, chickadees rustle and twitter among the snowy, dark branches.

As we near the Cathedral, we are joined on the road by neighbors in groups of two or three, and we nod and say hello without waving, unwilling to draw our hands from warm pockets. It's a relief to open the heavy wooden door and enter the warm, bright building that smells of incense. We shed coats and boots in the narthex and then take our places in the nave.

"Blessed is the kingdom of the Father and of the Son and of the Holy Spirit." With these words, our pastor, Fr. Marc, lifts the jeweled Gospel book and begins the prayers and hymns of the Liturgy.

It's hard to imagine our community without its heart and center, the Cathedral. Fr. Marc calls it our "living room," the place where we gather as God's family, and, like most of the other places on Monastery, it was planned and built and decorated by the community that lives here.

Here is a story of serendipity: In 1981, when the decision was made to build the Cathedral, the state of Alaska was flush with income from the Prudhoe-to-Valdez oil pipeline and founded the Permanent Fund, a savings account that is now worth multibillions of dollars. From the interest on the fund's earnings, we Alaskans receive a yearly check just for living here, and the first payout was $1,000 to each man, woman, and child. The members of the community pooled their Permanent Fund dividend checks and broke ground for a church.

The Cathedral is built in the shape of a cross. The altar faces east, the direction of the sunrise, which symbolizes the age to come. Instead of a steeple pointing to a distant heaven, the church is topped with a dome, which reminds us that God is present with us and that in our worship we are gathered in His warm embrace.

The building itself is an icon, a sacred image of the community that worships in it. Its three main parts are the narthex, or vestibule, which represents the world; the nave, where the people gather, which

23

represents the Church; and the sanctuary, in which stands the altar, representing the kingdom of heaven, the place toward which we and all Christians are always heading.

I stand in the nave and look up at the expansive ceiling, sixty feet across and covered with hand-milled Alaskan birch; at the inside of the cupola with its familiar image of Christ and the angels, painted by my friend Robin with the help of a group of children; at the glowing stained glass windows created by Anna and Keith and Tom; and, finally, at the icons, the "windows to heaven," surrounding the altar. Seeing our priests and deacons gathered in the apse, in front of the great Ascension icon with its images of the disciples standing in a semicircle behind them, it seems to me a visual reminder of the unbroken line of teaching that began two thousand years ago and continues to the present day.

Twenty-eight years after receiving my first Permanent Fund check, I have forgotten exactly how I spent mine. But I'm grateful to my St. John's neighbors—of whom I knew nothing back then—for their generosity that turned a dream into a splendid reality.

I bring my attention back to the present to listen as Fr. Marc reads the Gospel. When he is done, our next-door neighbor, Deacon Dan, strides to the lectern to deliver the homily, or sermon, for the Feast. As befits a retired U.S. Navy Commander, he speaks briskly and enthusiastically, without a trace of nervousness and with only an occasional glance at his notes.

When Mary and Joseph brought their son into the Temple that day, he says, two elderly people waited there to receive them. The righteous old priest Simeon saw prophecy being fulfilled right before his eyes. The elderly widow Anna actually lived in the Temple, where she prayed and fasted and waited to see the redemption of

Israel. Both Simeon and Anna were in the right place at the right time.

Dan was born in Normal, Illinois, a town that lives up to its name, but he realized early on that it was not the place where he wanted to spend his life. Like Simeon and Anna, Dan *knew* there was a place he needed to be, but it took a while to find it. Both he and his wife Theresa have an itch to wander, and his navy career made it possible for them to do just that.

Over the years, Dan and Theresa and their children changed churches along with duty stations—Nazarene, Vineyard Christian Fellowship, Lutheran, Roman Catholic—but it was during his Alaska assignment that he received a telephone call from an excited friend who'd read about a "convert" Orthodox church in Eagle River and urged him to check it out. This call led Dan and Theresa to Monastery Drive one frosty winter evening for their first Vespers service, and, eventually, to the sacraments of chrismation and, for Dan, ordination.

They sold their large, comfortable house and moved the family into a smaller, less convenient duplex on Monastery Drive. But it wasn't the real estate that attracted them. They wanted to live in a place where they could really get to know their neighbors and hear the church bells ring every day, reminding them why they are here in the first place.

We have been seated for Deacon Dan's homily. We stand as the service continues and a young couple brings their newborn son to the front of the nave for the Prayers of Naming. Just after their marriage in 1998, Midwesterners Kirk and Kim were living in Anchorage while they attended the University of Alaska. Kirk loves history and had done some reading about the Orthodox Church, so they attended a service at St. John's. Even though the church and the community immediately "felt like home," they chose to move back to Indiana, where they bought a house and started a family. Their first child's medical problems made them more serious about their faith, and eventually led to their chrismation into the Orthodox Church.

Kirk and Kim couldn't forget the closeness of the community at St. John's. They longed to raise their children in a home near the church and educate them in the community's small school. Eventually, everything, including a job and a house near Monastery Drive, fell into place, and once again, Kirk and Kim felt as if they had come home.

The Prayers of Naming, on the eighth day after a baby's birth, is one of the sweetest little services in the Orthodox Church. First, Fr. Marc thanks God for keeping Kim safe through childbearing (sometimes called the "churching" of the mother, which was traditionally done on the fortieth day after childbirth, but now is often done along with the prayer of naming). Then he prays for baby Oscar, "that he may flee from the vanity of the world and from every snare of the enemy." In the orderly Orthodox manner, Fr. Marc looks forward to Oscar's baptism and prays that he will "be united in due time to Your Holy Church."

Then comes the part that we all love to watch. Children squeeze through the crowd to get a better view as Fr. Marc takes baby Oscar from Kim's arms, carries him to the icon of the Mother of God, and lifts him before her eyes. "Rejoice, O Virgin Theotokos, full of grace . . ." He repeats the familiar words. "And rejoice also, O righteous elder, for you received in your arms the Redeemer of our souls."

This scene—Fr. Marc in gold vestments, reciting ancient prayers as he holds the infant in his arms—is what I imagine when I think of Mary and Joseph bringing their baby son into the Temple in Jerusalem for "presentation" to God.

The Divine Liturgy is almost over, and Fr. Marc and Deacon Dan bring the chalices of consecrated wine and bread from the altar and invite us to "draw near" and receive the Holy Eucharist. The first to draw near is a bearded, silver-haired man wearing a black cassock and a large gold cross around his neck. After he has received the sacrament, he returns to his place, greeting people along the way like a Baptist preacher at a Sunday potluck.

He is Harold Dunaway (now Fr. Harold), who was succeeded as pastor of St. John's Church by his son, Fr. Marc, and is retired from active ministry. Watching him make his way through the crowded nave, I recall a story I heard about another boy whose parents dedicated him to God. Fr. Harold knows a lot more than I do about how to get people to listen, so I will tell his story as he told it to me:

> I was born in Maysville, Kentucky, and I was a real river rat. I was raised in the Pentecostal Holiness Church, and my mother and dad were devout Christians. Dad wanted to go to China as a missionary, but Mom didn't want to leave Kentucky. So Dad took me to church and prayed that one day I would go out and be a missionary.
>
> Pentecostal Holiness was a straitlaced religion—no working on Sundays, women wore no makeup, that sort of thing. I didn't want to live under that law, so I ran away and joined the Army when I was fifteen. But they found out I was too young and shipped me home. I served in Korea, eventually got out of the Army and went to Albuquerque, where I sold insurance.
>
> I called myself an agnostic back then. I was taking some classes at the University of New Mexico, sitting around with some other students, discussing God and His existence. And I made the remark that just to prove there was no God, He could strike me dead right then. Now *that's* flirting. I have said many times since then, if I had been God, I would have killed me. And if it wasn't for the grace of God, I don't know what would have happened.

Barbara, who is also from Maysville, and I got married during the Albuquerque years. Raymond, our neighbor across the street, was a butcher. I met him at the gym—we played handball together—and we became close friends. He was an Independent Baptist, and he kept on witnessing to me, and I made fun of him, in a gentle sort of way. I told him, "Man, if I believed everything you're telling me, I wouldn't be selling meat. I'd be out there telling the whole world." That went on for a year.

One afternoon, I was lying on my couch, a glass of wine in one hand and a cigarette in the other, enjoying my afternoon off. Raymond knocked on the door and came in with a Bible in his hand. He said, "Would you do me one favor? Would you read this right here?" I said I would, and I read it out loud: "If you will confess with your mouth the Lord Jesus Christ and believe in your heart that God has raised Him from the dead, you shall be saved."

Now, it was never my intention to "get saved." But that afternoon I believe I came to Jesus Christ by irresistible grace. I did not make a decision—it was made for me. That's the way I look at it.

I was baptized and joined Raymond's church, and pretty soon they made me a Sunday School teacher. From the day I was saved, for the next twelve years, I fought going into the ministry. I had a good job. I was making a lot of money. I was the top salesman for my company every year. God was calling me to do something else, but I kept saying no.

In the mid-sixties, we moved back to Kentucky, just outside Lexington. I met a fellow by the name of Jay Kulina, the director of Campus Crusade for Christ at the University of Kentucky. One day Jay asked if he could use my house for a meeting of college students. I said yes, and we had the meeting, and I got excited.

All those years I had thought God wanted me to be a preacher. One day I was in my brand-spanking-new green Volkswagen and I was talking out loud to God, as I usually did. I said, "God, I'm tired of fighting You. I give up. What do You want me to do?" When I got home I told Barbara that I wanted to go on staff with Campus Crusade, and I asked her what she thought of that. She said okay.

Now, to go on staff, I either had to have a college education or a seminary degree. I had neither. But I figured I could get through seminary a lot quicker than through college, so I told Barbara we were going to seminary.

In 1966, we lived on a farm outside Lexington, with big black walnut trees and three cars in the driveway. We sold everything except one car, rented a little U-Haul, and headed for Bible Baptist College in Springfield, Missouri. We drove around town and saw a nice apartment building. I went in and told the manager we were looking for a place to live. He said that I would be his maintenance man and we would get our rent in exchange for unplugging toilets and scraping food off the walls. I kept the swimming pool clean and moved furniture. If somebody moved out and left food in the freezer, we ate it. So the job had benefits.

In 1968, I had my seminary degree, and we moved again, this time to the Campus Crusade headquarters in California for training. I was assigned to the military division, and I figured they would send me to either Washington, D.C., or Pensacola, Florida. One day they handed me a sealed envelope, and when we opened it, I found out I was posted to Anchorage, Alaska. It was a shock, and I could have said no. I thought it over for a couple of days and decided to take it.

When we got to Anchorage, we had seventeen dollars. We spent the first night at the Wonder Park Hotel, then moved into an apartment on Government Hill, close to the military bases. My usual daily routine was to go to the Tap Room, a little café on Fort Richardson, buy a soft drink, and find guys to talk to. I used the Campus Crusade conversation starter—I would ask them to participate in a little survey, and if they said yes, I would talk to them about what Crusade called the Four Spiritual Laws. I wasn't bashful—once I prayed with a G.I. under the flagpole at Ft. Rich. I spent eighty percent of my time at Ft. Rich and twenty percent at Elmendorf Air Force Base.

Our little apartment got crowded in a hurry. G.I.s and their friends were dropping in to talk and coming over to study the Bible together. A supporter of ours who was a businessman made me a proposition: He would supply us with land and materials if we would build a house. Those G.I.s started working, and soon we had a bigger place to live in east Anchorage at 405 Fern Street.

Young people were leaving the churches to come join us, and that did not make some of the pastors too happy. Sometimes the pastors would come to our meetings, but none of them seemed to understand the attraction. They had us figured for some kind of commune.

One day I was called to a meeting at the Hilton Hotel in Anchorage. I knocked on the door and was met by a representative from Campus Crusade and eight local pastors. There was no place for me to sit, so I sat on the radiator while they grilled me about what I was teaching to the kids who were leaving their churches and coming to me. Later, the Crusade rep told me to be careful about offending the local pastors. It was then I decided to resign my position with Campus Crusade.

What I wanted was to disciple converts, to find a place where I could gather a group of people and study the Bible and find out together what God's will was for us. I had a family to support, so I created a nonprofit corporation and called it Maranatha North. We found a big house on five acres in Eagle River, and it looked perfect for us, but we heard it had already been sold. All this was happening in 1971.

Around this same time, I met and talked with a visiting evangelist named Jack Archer. I told him about the Eagle River property, and he suggested we go and look at it together and talk to the realtor. I was amazed to find out that the property was back on the market. The realtor said it would take five thousand dollars upfront for us to buy it. Jack Archer wrote a check for five thousand dollars on the spot. So I guess you could say that's how we found our home.

Now, everyone has received communion, the Liturgy is over, and Fr. Marc holds the heavy gold blessing cross while each of us stands in front of him, waiting our turn to kiss first the cross and then his hand that holds it. In return, I hear his murmured words that I love so much: "The Lord bless you, Mary Alice."

Kissing things—icons, crosses, a priest's hand—can be tough for Protestant converts. From babyhood, my faithful parents made sure I was nourished on Baptist dogma, and the warnings to "worship no graven image" and to remember "the priesthood of the believer" were staples. At the chrismation service for a friend, one of the first Orthodox services I ever attended, I watched as the line formed in front of the priest and I thought, "I believe I will be able to kiss his cross, but I will never kiss his hand."

But I did kiss his hand, and I wasn't struck dead on the spot. Since then, I have gradually come to understand that bowing before an icon and kissing a priest's hand are acts of respect, not worship, and are mysterious channels of grace which I still only dimly understand.

"Happy Feast Day!" Fr. Marc sends us to the downstairs social hall, where we will find hot coffee and treats, neighbors and visitors to greet, and our first close-up look at little Oscar. Seeing him nestled in Kirk's arms reminds me of my own sons and why this day is special for our family. It is the anniversary of our chrismation.

Our oldest son, who at first did not share his parents' enthusiasm for conversion, told me later that when he was away from home during his college years and often unable to attend services, he missed the hymn of St. Simeon most of all, the hymn that was first sung at the Presentation of the Lord: "Lord, now You are letting Your servant depart in peace, according to Your word. For my eyes have seen Your salvation which You have prepared before the face of all peoples: a light to enlighten the Gentiles and the glory of Your people, Israel."

I have always loved time travel stories, especially the part where one tiny thing is altered in the past, changing *everything* in the future. People who need to get married wind up never even meeting, and babies who need to be born vanish from history. When I apply this fantasy scenario to my own life, and that of my family and neighbors at St. John's, I think: How would God have worked out our salvation if Harold and Barbara had chosen to refuse their assignment to Alaska?

But they did not refuse it. They chose to say yes, setting in motion a complex sequence of events, like those hundreds of dominoes that are painstakingly arranged and then tipped to fall in an intricate pattern. Because one did *this*, another does *that*. Harold and Barbara go to Alaska, and a community is born. A friend makes a phone call, and Dan becomes an Orthodox deacon. Two people meet in a classroom, and I move to a new home. It is by this mysterious grace that God works, and allows us to work out, our salvation.

God has willed that we should all depend on one another for our salvation, and all strive together for our own mutual good and our own common salvation.

—THOMAS MERTON

The Big House in Maranatha North days, circa 1972

Early Big House residents clown for the camera.

Gathering in the Big House living room, circa 1975

Fr. Harold baptizes Joseph Lamb in the Chugiak High School pool, 1980.

St. John's Cathedral construction: Raising a gable end

Framing the dome

Top:
Snowball fight
during
construction

Bottom:
Erecting the cross
atop the dome

Chrismation of St. John's Orthodox Church, 1987

Left to right: Archdeacon Hans, Fr. Jack Sparks, Metropolitan Philip, and Fr. Harold Dunaway, on the day of St. John's chrismations (photo by Dianne Cranor)

The clergy of St. John's gathered at Pascha

Top:
St John's School
students and staff

Bottom:
Fr. Marc reads to the
children on St. Sergius
Day.

St. Sergius Chapel

Yuri Sidorenko painting the icons for St. Sergius Chapel

Fr. Lazarus Moore seated in the Big House in front of his portrait

Visit of
Patriarch
Alexy II in
1993

Monk Innocent (great-grandson of St. Innocent of Irkutsk) with children, 1989

School children sledding on the hill between the Big House and the school

St. John's neighbors stay warm at a winter bonfire.

Girls headed to St. John's annual summer youth camp

A Pascha gathering at the cemetery

Fr. Marc and school children making a procession to St. Sergius Chapel

Grammy Phyl's funeral procession

Top:
Fr. Harold & Barbara's
50th anniversary

Bottom:
Harold and Barbara P.
on their wedding day

Steve dressed in
performance regalia

Tim and Tanna's
wedding

Top:
Robin in her
iconography studio
at the Cathedral

Bottom:
Rosalie and Al on
a picnic with their
children; Al's brother
Phil is at center.

AN INTERRUPTION OF LIFE

MARCH

FEAST OF THE ANNUNCIATION

Today is the beginning of our salvation and the revelation of the mystery which is from eternity: The Son of God becomes the Son of the Virgin, and Gabriel proclaims good tidings of grace. Let us, therefore, cry out with him to the Mother of God, Rejoice, you who are full of grace, the Lord is with you! —TROPARION OF THE FEAST

MARCH IN ALASKA IS A LONG, LONG MONTH. MAYBE THAT'S why the Church decided to put most of Lent in it. I'm joking—even cranky sourdoughs like me can find plenty to be glad about in March. On a bright blue and gold day last week, in the middle of some errands in Anchorage, our good old dog Axel and I took a walk around Goose Lake. The trail is right smack in the middle of the city, but I swear there are places on it where you feel as if you are alone in a primeval forest during the melting of the first ice age.

Anyway, the walk allowed me to slow down and notice that the sun was no longer crouched low on the horizon but was perched high in the sky, and when I turned my face up to it, my cheeks and closed eyelids felt warm. Then I opened my eyes and saw that even though the birch branches are still bare, they are no longer thin and colored winter gray, but are promisingly fuller, and the swelling leaf buds have turned them a reddish color. It felt good to be alive, to be glad that I have climbed the high snowy hill of winter and now I'm coasting down the other side.

On this afternoon a week later, the sun is still shining, but a biting wind has kicked up, swirling snow from the rooftops and chasing us up and down Monastery Drive. Today is Forgiveness Sunday, the start of Great Lent and the Great Fast (yes, indeed, there is a reason those words are capitalized).

I dash through the stinging wind to my friend Robin's house. Robin is a Southern lady, an artist, a book lover, a seeker of God. After earning an art degree in Georgia, she backpacked around Europe and dropped in one day at a little community she had heard of in the mountains of Switzerland. It was L'Abri (a French word that means *shelter*), the Christian community founded by Dr. Francis and Edith Schaeffer, the very place that Barbara Dunaway had read about and dreamed of recreating in Alaska.

Mrs. Schaeffer invited Robin to stay for awhile and she did, living in one of the little chalets, helping out in the kitchen, studying Christianity in the L'Abri way, with the help of tapes recorded by Dr. Schaeffer. Robin showed me a book, a pictorial story of L'Abri during the 1960s, and there she is in one of the pictures, standing in the Schaeffers' living room in intense conversation with a young man. Except for her long hair and sixties-style dress, she looks like the same Robin that I know and love today.

She stayed at L'Abri for six months and recalls the interesting people she met, the stimulating conversation, and the hospitality of Mrs. Schaeffer, who insisted that at every meal the table should be properly set for her family and guests. L'Abri was a celebrated place, a community but not a church, sought out by the famous and the unknown. It received wayfarers, let them stay for a time, taught them what it could, and then sent them on their way.

Robin remembers her time there with fondness and gratitude, and acknowledges the similarities between L'Abri and the community at St. John's, but the most telling difference, she believes, is that the center of St. John's is not the hospitality or the conversation or the teaching—though all these are highly prized. Here, rather, is the Church, its life-giving sacraments and its changeless worship. Just as at L'Abri, folks come to visit our community, many decide to stay, and others choose to leave. But the Church is permanent.

After her European adventure, Robin went back to Augusta, Georgia—her hometown—and taught school for awhile. In Augusta she joined a Protestant church community that was, coincidentally, connected with the same Pilgrim Holiness movement in which Harold Dunaway was raised. The teaching there leaned toward legalism, and the people observed a long list of dos and don'ts. She tried to follow all the rules, but eventually became restless and ready to move on again.

Robin decided to visit her sister, who lived in Anchorage. Within days of her arrival, she accepted an invitation from an acquaintance to visit the Big House in Eagle River, where she listened gratefully to Harold Dunaway's teaching about God's grace. Over thirty years later, she still lives in the community that first formed in the Big House on Monastery Drive.

After the community's conversion to Orthodoxy, Robin became its resident iconographer. Her icons and banners decorate not only our Cathedral, but many other churches and homes as well. Her most recent large project, a series of icons of the twelve Great Feasts, adorns the top of the iconostasis she created for the newly built Cathedral. She can be found most weekdays in her crowded little studio, surrounded by books and icons and paints and brushes, her latest project propped before her on the work table.

Gale arrived on the scene not long after Robin. He is a professional pilot, a Civil War buff, and a wood craftsman. He builds oak coffins that are simple and beautiful, and keeps one or two on hand, in his workshop, just in case. He met Robin, who later became his wife, at the hospital where they both worked, and she brought him to visit the Big House community. He was, he says, a "backslid Protestant Christian" at the time, and the people and the community looked good to him, so he stayed.

Gale told me how they put meat on the Big House table in those days. The state of Alaska, both then and now, keeps a list of nonprofit groups that are eligible to receive the carcasses of road-killed moose on state highways. The Big House group was on the roadkill list, and when it was their turn, somebody had to go and haul away the carcass. Gale was the only person around who owned a pickup, so when the call came, he had to find some helpers and go get the dead moose, then hang it in the garage for butchering. Telling me his story, Gale looked over the top of his glasses and, in his deadpan way, explained that moose hardly ever get run over on clear, dry days. No, he says, they usually get hit at night, in sub-freezing temperatures, in the rain or snow. It's not a pretty picture.

Robin is a friend who shares her life generously. I arrive shivering at her door, and she makes me a cup of tea and says she is glad that Lent is here. After the steady feasting since Christmas that puts many of us in a winter malaise, she welcomes Lent's demand for discipline, its structure of services, and its call for quiet reflection.

But I didn't pop in at Robin's just to chat over a cup of tea. She has been up and down for weeks with a persistent flu, and I am nagged uncomfortably by the fact that I have neglected her. I have come to confess my shortcomings and to ask for her forgiveness. She, of course, forgives me lovingly and immediately. After promising to try harder to be a better friend, I hug her and leave with that lightness of spirit that always accompanies confession, no matter how small the transgression may seem.

We talked about this very thing at reading group the other night—the difficulty that goes hand-in-hand with the pleasure of living close together in a church (or for that matter, any) community. For years, a group of friends has met off and on to read together and talk generally about life and particularly about our own lives. Robin, who was once an English teacher, is usually our leader. Lesa, Maye, Maris, Doreen, Theresa, Annie, Nancy, and I have moved in and out of the group as our lives permit. We occasionally bring our husbands, along with a bottle of wine and a plate of snacks, and socialize together, sometimes reading and sometimes just talking.

Anyway, the other night, Nancy, a smart and outspoken lady who relishes wrestling with difficult topics, started a discussion about the trials of living in close community with people who behave badly, who are difficult to like, who are constantly needy. After a lot of back-and-forth talk, Nancy joked that maybe the best way to "survive" living in community is to simply accept that there are people here we will always struggle to like, and to let it go at that.

In her gentle, sensible way, Maris reminded us of a story that we read together, "The Enormous Radio" by John Cheever, about a couple whose life together is a "satisfactory average of income, endeavor and respectability." But their orderly existence is disturbed when the wife hears, via a new radio, her neighbors' private conversations. At first she laughs at their complaints and petty arguments, and then cries over their sickness and misfortune. She is curious about them, but she makes no effort to get involved in their lives.

Gradually, she becomes hooked on listening in, and then worried that the neighbors can hear what is going on in her own house. She begs her husband to reassure her that they, at least, have "never been like that . . . we've always been good and decent and loving to one another."

Finally, fed up with his wife's obsession, the husband explodes. "Why are you so Christly all of a sudden?" he sarcastically asks her before reciting a list of her secret sins, from stealing her sister's inheritance to a secret abortion. His wife is humiliated, and she silently turns off the radio.

Maris wondered if we are like the woman in the story, that we prefer to avoid too much intimacy with our neighbors and, aside from a certain curiosity about their lives, would rather not know the unpleasant details. And like her, we'd prefer that our neighbors see only the side of our lives that we choose to show them.

People often visit our church and community, Maris said, and at first, they like what they find. It's nice and warm and welcoming, and they think they want to stay. But eventually the time comes when they are called on to open up a bit to others—to be *real*—and that is not quite as nice as just being comfortable.

Nancy agreed and suggested that it is also the pretty side of our community that we want to show to the world—the children playing happily together on the church lawn, the socializing together at picnics and potlucks, our enjoyment of the beauty of Alaska that is literally right outside our doors. She added, of course, that it is all delightful, and we are blessed.

But she went further. *Real* community, she said, is made up of real people, and it is sometimes messier than these pictures suggest. In a real community, people do not necessarily "like" everyone else. At times, some neighbors are strong and giving; at others they are weak and needy. The demands of caring for the needy ones can grow burdensome.

The people in our community get divorced, struggle with depression and addiction, and disappoint each other regularly. Young, unmarried girls face unplanned pregnancies, businesses go bankrupt, and children defy their parents' rules and standards. And sometimes we just plain get on each others' nerves.

As I recall that reading group discussion, I think about a neighbor—I'll call her Sarah—whom I did *not* visit this afternoon. Asking Robin's forgiveness was easy—we are close friends, and her generous spirit is well known to me, along with her willingness to reprove me (gently) when necessary. But my out-of-line behavior has offended someone else in the community, someone who is not a warm, cozy friend, and our relationship has been cold for weeks.

Whenever my path crosses Sarah's, her averted eyes remind me of the unspoken tension between us, and my feelings of sadness are mixed with reassurances to myself that my behavior was justified, that I am not the only one at fault. Since I have less invested in my relationship with her than I do with, for instance, Robin, it has become easy to avert my eyes as well and to let the matter lie there, quietly festering.

Sarah is the person I really need to talk to. I am uncomfortably aware of my unwillingness to get real.

THAT NIGHT, THE COMMUNITY GATHERS IN THE CATHEDRAL for the Vespers of Forgiveness Sunday. The service begins as usual until, about halfway through, things start to change. Deacon Dan begins to chant the litanies, the prayers of petition, in a different, minor key, and our response of "Lord, have mercy" sounds different as well. Then we hear the first notes of the prokeimenon (a refrain sung responsively to introduce a scripture reading) with its plaintive plea, "Turn not away Your face from Your child, for I am afflicted . . ." On cue, the overhead chandeliers are switched off completely (they will not be lighted again until Easter morning), and the service continues in the now dimly lit nave.

At this point the children, who may have been fussy or distracted, look up to watch as Fr. Marc and Deacon Dan transform themselves and the altar from everyday coverings to Lenten ones. They take off their gold vestments and put on robes of deep purple. Slowly and methodically, they remove everything from the altar—the Gospel in its gold and jeweled binding, the heavy candlesticks, and the Tabernacle, the special container in which is kept the reserved Eucharist—and drape the altar in a purple cloth before putting everything back in its place.

And then it is time for the yearly ritual of the forgiveness circle. Fr. Marc tells us to form two large circles, one inside the other, with a loop on the end. For the next hour, the circles move from left to right and from right to left, and, one by one, we come face-to-face with each of our fellow parishioners.

I find my place in the circle and say to my neighbor across from me, "Will you please forgive me?" Though I do not list them, I am asking him to forgive me for all the offenses, voluntary and involuntary, open and hidden, which I have committed against him in the previous year. He replies to me, "I forgive you. Will you forgive me?" "Yes," I say, "God forgives all." We exchange a hug and move to the next person in line, and we don't stop until each person has come face-to-face with every other person in the circle.

When it is over, I slip out of the church into the cold dark night and trudge home, choosing not to stay in the bright light of the narthex to chat with my neighbors. Tonight, for the first time in seventeen years, I do not feel the lightness of spirit that I have always felt after the forgiveness circle.

I wish I could tell you that I went to Sarah's house this afternoon, that I confessed my wrong and asked for her forgiveness, and that when we met in the circle, there was no longer a barrier between us. But I didn't. Instead, I allowed my pride to keep me from doing what I knew was right. And when I stood across from her, I tried to believe that the words and hug we exchanged were enough to set everything right. But I don't think they were.

The next day, the first day of the Fast, is called by the Church "Clean Monday." I love the promising sound of it, like new beginnings and fresh starts. At Compline that night, we will say the ancient prayer of St. Ephraim, a penitential plea that sums up the spirit of Lent and is prayed, accompanied by prostrations, all through the forty days of the Fast:

> O Lord and Master of my life,
> Do not give to me the spirit of laziness,
> Faintheartedness, lust for power and idle talk;
> But give rather the spirit of chastity, humility,
> Patience and love to Your servant.

O Lord and King, grant me to see my own faults
And not to judge my brother,
For blessed are You unto ages of ages.

Henri Nouwen, a Catholic priest/author whose books are favorites of our reading group, says in *Behold the Beauty of the Lord*, "It is hard for us to relinquish our worldly identity as noteworthy people and accept our spiritual identity as children of God. We so much want to be looked at that we are ill prepared to be truly seen."

Barbara Dunaway might have had this very thought in mind when, in an early Big House newsletter, she wrote, "Community is a reflecting place, a mirror of ourselves and our way of living, showing us through exchanges with brothers and sisters in common faith how our thoughts and lifestyles affect them by our selfish and unselfish actions."

Maybe the definition of "real community" is this: It is a place where, if people stay long enough and feel safe enough, they can slowly begin to drop their masks and reveal themselves, with increasing honesty, to at least one or two, maybe more, people. And perhaps those who are fortunate enough to find "real community" receive a blessing far beyond anything for which they could have dared to ask or hope.

TWO WEEKS AFTER FORGIVENESS SUNDAY, OUR DRIED-OUT Christmas trees are burning up in a blaze of glory at a St. Patrick's Day bonfire. We are here to honor the great saint of the West, who, on Easter Sunday in 433, defied the Irish king's order to light no fires by kindling a huge one on the Hill of Slane. We drag our brittle Christmas trees and wreaths to the firepit and toss them in one by one, each producing a brief but awesome blaze, and the kids imagine that ours, like

St. Patrick's, can be seen from miles away. Our neighbor John, a tall soft-spoken fellow who looks more like a tweedy professor than the civil servant he actually is, tells the story of the life of St. Patrick, and we listen, transfixed in the glow of the fire.

Every year, St. Patrick's Day lands somewhere during Lent, but it is not the only feast that interrupts the Great Fast in March. The Feast of the Annunciation celebrates the angel Gabriel's announcement to Mary, a young, unmarried Hebrew woman, that she was chosen to give birth to the Son of God. In the icons, the direct intervention of the Holy Spirit into everyday life is depicted as a golden ray shooting into the picture at the top edge of the canvas. The ray signals that the heavenly kingdom has broken into earthly time and space. That is what the announcement to Mary was like; her life was interrupted by bewildering news that was difficult to understand, let alone assent to.

Generally speaking, folks don't take kindly to interruptions. No matter how many times we hear that Bible verse about "entertaining angels unaware," it's hard to drag our attention away from what we are doing, especially when it is to focus on another's need, even if she does turn out to be an angel.

Fr. Marc often advises his parishioners to embrace change. "Change," he says, "is how we grow." And he should know—he was a teenager when his life was upended by his dad's Campus Crusade assignment to Alaska. Seventh grade is tough, let alone going into it in a new school in a place far from the familiar.

If you knew Fr. Marc, I think you would agree with me that he is a cool, calm, and collected man. But in ninth grade, he says, he "freaked out" after his dad resigned from Crusade and the family moved into the Fern Street house. He was tired of Alaska, tired of the people crowding into his house, tired of others' claims on his parents' time and attention. We need a break, he told his dad, and Harold listened. He took the family on a two-month camping trip to the Lower Forty-eight.

I asked Fr. Marc if he ever worried that he had interrupted his parents' work. "No," he told me matter-of-factly. "They interrupted my life." And he meant it.

Sometimes interruptions come crashing into our lives like King Kong trampling a trail through the jungle. During Lent several years ago, a space of only forty days, a series of events shook our community and left us reeling: Deacon Christian and Kent, both of them husbands and fathers of young children, died suddenly and were buried, just three weeks apart; my dear friend Rosalie endured chemotherapy for breast cancer and worried about the future of her husband Al and their three young daughters; Robert, another father of young children, suffered stroke-like symptoms; and Nancy's teenaged son lost part of a finger in a freak snowboarding accident.

Humans, whether Christian or not, are usually at a loss to explain or understand that kind of rapid-fire sorrow, and the fact that we live in a close church community does not make us any different. But I am here to tell you that there is a great deal of comfort to be found in living in the presence of others who, in spite of the fact that they cannot always explain things to you, can and do offer each other comfort, encouragement, and support.

Robin knows about such interruptions, about news that comes crashing into one's world and immediately changes everything. Ten years ago, she and her husband Gale were comfortably settled in their new house. They had raised two children, and Robin was happily devoting herself to painting icons when word came that her sister Jackie, the mother of young twin boys, was terminally ill—would Robin and Gale care for the boys after Jackie's death? For the next eight years, through good times and challenging times, Robin and Gale parented the boys and loved them as their own sons, willingly putting many aspects of their own lives on hold for a season. That's what families do.

Fifteen years ago, unexpected and frightening news crashed into my family's world, forcing us way out of our comfort zone and into the world of doctors, hospitals, and uncertainty. Our oldest son Adam had finished his first year of college and was back at home for the summer. On a gorgeous, sunny morning in July, Adam, Bill, and I walked down the road to church and took our places just as the Liturgy was beginning.

Suddenly, Adam fell to the floor. Bill and I knelt beside him, and I recall my husband's frightened face as he told me to go to the phone and call 911. The prayers continued for a minute or two after Adam collapsed, but as I ran from the nave, I was aware of complete silence.

While I was gone, my head cleared enough so that I could think. Was my son dying? Was he already dead? How was it possible that a young man who had appeared to be so healthy minutes before could now appear so lifeless? My hands and voice shook as I spoke to the emergency dispatcher.

I hurried back and found Adam in the same position, surrounded by Rita, a nurse, Gordon, a paramedic, and Irene, a doctor. Bill's fear had turned into barely suppressed panic, and Fr. Paul (a dear priest who has since become pastor of a church in Homer, Alaska) knelt beside him, praying. People spoke in whispers, and we all waited helplessly until the EMTs arrived and wheeled Adam to the ambulance for the fifteen-minute ride to the nearest hospital.

Our faithful friends Al and Rosalie put Bill and me—dazed and shaken—in their truck and followed the ambulance to Anchorage.

At the hospital, it did not take long to receive a diagnosis: grand mal seizure, cause unknown. Adam was given anti-seizure medication and kept under observation for several hours. We took him home and put him to bed; I tiptoed into his room several times that night and leaned close to his face to make sure that he still breathed, as if he were an infant again and not a young man.

An MRI revealed clearly the cause: A slow-growing tumor in the right temporal lobe of his brain had enlarged to the point that it triggered a seizure. The neurologist recommended that we seek the advice of a neurosurgeon. Although shaken by his words, we had a diagnosis and could begin to move toward treatment and, God willing, a cure. During the next few weeks, I welcomed the need to remain focused on finding for our son the best surgeon at the best hospital; activity allowed me to keep the words *brain tumor* on the periphery of my mind.

Two months later, a second seizure forced us into a decision. We took Adam to Methodist Hospital in Houston, Texas, and entrusted him to the care of Dr. Robert Grossman, a neurosurgeon who had helped treat President Kennedy in the emergency room at Parkland Hospital in Dallas, and now specializes in the surgical treatment of epilepsy.

Bill and I grew up in a culture that encouraged families to hang together in a crisis, so all five of us traveled to Houston to support Adam and each other. Texas relatives rallied around us as well, and five thousand miles from our St. John's community, we felt its nearness—its prayers and its love—every single day.

It is here that Adam's story intersects with another one, about another community. Later, when the time is right, I will pick up the threads of both and try to show how each of them offered us a chance to grow in our faith in God and in His Church.

Like Mary, when she was surprised by the angel Gabriel, each of us will be confronted with circumstances and choices that are confusing, difficult to see a way through, and impossible to know the outcome of. Like yours, my reaction is often fear and the quickly asked question, "Why me?" But by God's grace and with the encouragement of a loving, believing community—and though it may take a lifetime—each of us, like Mary, can learn to say, "Let it be done to me according to Your will."

If it is good to know oneself, then it is twice good to know oneself in the presence of others. —Anonymous

IT TAKES A VILLAGE

APRIL

PALM SUNDAY

*Seated upon the throne in heaven and upon the colt on earth, O Christ
our God, You did accept the praise of the angels and the songs of the children who cried out to You, Blessed are You who come to recall Adam from
the dead.* —KONTAKION OF THE FEAST

APRIL IS THE CRUELEST MONTH . . .

That was all I could remember, so I looked it up and found that
it is the first line of T.S. Eliot's *The Waste Land*. Here is what he said:

April is the cruelest month, breeding
Lilacs out of the dead land, mixing
Memory and desire, stirring
Dull roots with spring rain.

There must be a reason those words kept running through my
head, I thought. Maybe I should write a poem of my own, an Alaskan
version:

COMMUNITY OF GRACE

April is the cruelest month, breeding
Thoughts of never-ending winter, mixing
Dreams of sun-drenched beaches, stirring
Tired bodies with unwelcome snow.

My little effort at parody made me feel quite clever and relieved some of my yearly frustration at living in a sub-Arctic (barely) climate zone, where the landscape is not in synch with my childhood memories of fields of April bluebonnets and trees exploding in green leafiness.

Spring in Alaska is different from spring in the Lower Forty-eight. When the daylight hours on Monastery Drive start to lengthen and the ice on our roofs drips steadily from the eaves, I begin to look for signs that it is time to begin a yearly ritual I call "chopping the driveway." It's a strange family tradition, but it has become part of our history, one of the shared inside jokes that we laugh about while outsiders wonder what we find so funny.

When the glacier on the driveway begins to recede and water trickles away from it in little streams, I grab my chopping tool (it looks like a flat-bladed garden hoe) and hack around the glacier's edges. If I'm lucky, the ice comes away in big, satisfying chunks, and, like a deckhand on the Titanic, I shovel away the debris. I continue chopping at the ice until I reach a thickness that is resistant to the blade, and I know I have gone as far as I can go that day. When I stop, the driveway looks like an excavation site in Antarctica, but I am satisfied because I know that in just a few days we will once again be walking on dry pavement.

When my boys were small, I hoped to inspire them with my love of a clean driveway and, in their innocence, they happily helped me chop. Later, of course, as they became teenagers, they could not be either cajoled or forced into joining me because they were simply too busy. Now that they are grown, their amusement at my weird pastime is mixed with nostalgia. When the time is right, even if they are in some far-flung place where the temperature is in the comfortable 70° range, they will give me a call and say, laughing but serious, "Hey, Mom, are you chopping the driveway yet?" If I say yes, they know that it is springtime in Alaska.

Children love and need tradition, order, and predictability. The value of a tradition lies in its repetition, its intimacy, in the knowledge that this is what we do, what we have been through together, what we have shared, laughed at, and been a part of.

Speaking of kids and tradition, most of our kids refer to their parish as, simply, "the community," but a few have another name for it—*the Village*. It is impossible, of course, for adults to ever fully understand what transpires among teenagers, but as near as I can tell after quizzing my son Travis and his friends, *the Village* came into use at the local high school around ten years ago and was first coined, not pejoratively by a critic, but affectionately by a St. John's kid. The term caught on and eventually moved into the mainstream lingo. To this day, the kids at Chugiak High understand what is meant when they hear that one of their peers is "from the Village."

Mara, who graduated from Chugiak High five years ago, is a bright, articulate young lady who, when asked to write about her perception of growing up in the St. John's community, expressed her thoughts so beautifully that I decided to repeat them here in her own words:

I grew up in The Community. Not just any community, but The Community—capital T, capital C. Even in our local high school,

51

we kids who grew up attending Saint John's Orthodox Cathedral were known as the kids who were a part of The Community. I must admit, there were times when I almost hated disclosing the fact that I was a part of it. People know us, and they know what we stand for. There are expectations and standards which go along with being a part of The Community.

This makes me remember a party I went to during my freshman year of college. At this particular party, I ran into two kids I went to high school with. I was crammed onto a couch with them, a beer in one of my hands. "Mara, you drink?!? I thought you went to that one church?" one of them shouted in my ear. "Yeah, I go to that church," I said. Then I added, abruptly and awkwardly, "But I also can do whatever I want." She just stared at me with a puzzled look, and turned to talk to the next person.

I have looked back on that dialogue quite a few times since it happened. I wonder now why I was so defensive about being questioned about my behavior. I guess I almost hated admitting that, yes, I was a part of "that church." I think I was attempting to emphasize that even though I am an active Christian, I still have the freedom to do whatever I choose. But also, when I look back, I feel like I was ruining this certain ideal for the kid at the party. Because I was there, partying alongside of them, made it okay. I now see that because I was participating, I was giving The Community, and myself, kind of a bad name.

I think that moment was a learning experience for me. I finally realized that God happily allows me to be free, yet yearns for me to always make the right choices with that freedom. Every day I am discovering a little more about myself and about the different roles I play: I am a student, employee, sister, daughter, girlfriend, roommate, and an Orthodox Christian. While defining who I am in these roles, I am coming to understand that I cannot fulfill them all to their highest standards. All I can do is be me and seek God in all things.

I am starting to understand how my church is my family, too. Sometimes, I want to give up and run away. Being a part of this family can be hard. I just want to ditch out on all of the services, functions, and gatherings that go along with being a part of the church and do what I want, when I want to do it.

But then there are times when I am lost and feel lonely and isolated. I go from school, to work, and then home to my apartment, and feel like something is missing. These are the times I can go back to my parents' house, which is in the heart of The Community. I pop in and say hi and take a stroll up to the church. I run into neighbors and we talk, and they tell me how much they have missed seeing me and want to know all about my life. Sometimes I feel such intense joy to be a part of my church, an excitement and pride in being a part of this family. I am never lonely with them.

I may be learning this a little more slowly than others, but I really have no reason to feel the isolation that sometimes bears down on me. I have so many people eager to welcome me home, back into The Community. I don't always get along with everyone or want to be around that much. Yet there is this strange love that I have never found anywhere else, a kind of support and structure that is only found in a loving family. A sense of strength and independence empowers me when I realize that I can step out into the world all alone. But then I realize that being all alone in the world is not really what I want. I want to share my life with my family, who are always there to support and encourage me.

I guess the old African proverb is right—it really *does* take a village to raise a child.

I HAVE OFTEN WONDERED WHY THE PERSON WHO WROTE the troparion for Palm Sunday saw fit to make special mention of "the *children* who cried out to You." Why were they singled out from what must have been a very big crowd?

In St. Matthew's account of Jesus' memorable entrance into Jerusalem, just before His crucifixion, he mentions that there were "children crying out in the Temple and saying 'Hosanna to the Son of David.'" They must have followed Jesus there, because St. Matthew goes on to say that the Pharisees were really irritated by these kids and complained to Jesus, maybe expecting that, out of humility, He would shut up the little troublemakers. But He declined to do that. Instead, He praised them, in words that many of us still use (at least the first part) when we hear a child, or any innocent person, say something that seems wise beyond their years. "Out of the mouths of babes and nursing infants," Jesus said, "You have perfected praise."

It must have taken guts for those kids to stand within earshot of the lordly Pharisees (who were probably already planning how to take care of their "Jesus problem") and shout out those words of praise. Maybe St. Matthew had these children in mind when he told of a question the disciples asked Jesus. Who, they wanted to know, is greatest in the kingdom of God? (Reminds me of when my boys would bring their crayon pictures and Play-doh sculptures and ask me to tell them which one was the best. Humans seem to have an urgent need to determine who among them is first, best, greatest, etc.) Jesus called over a small child and then told the disciples, "Unless you are converted and become as little children, you will by no means enter the kingdom of heaven."

Jill, a young mother who grew up in the St. John's community and is now bringing up five children of her own, tells a story about two little ones, Anatoli and Andrew, and a quiet man, Andrew's father, who became Anatoli's "angel."

When she was eighteen years old, Jill woke up in a dark and confusing place that she did not at first realize was a hospital intensive care unit. She was told that she had experienced a grand mal seizure after a head injury, and had lost consciousness for a day and a half. She remained in the hospital for almost three weeks.

Meanwhile, a few floors away in the same hospital, a baby boy named Andrew lay in his little isolette, surrounded by tubes, electrodes, and monitors, fighting for his life. The meningitis that had attacked his body had caused fluid to create pressure in his brain. His parents, Harold (not to be confused with Harold Dunaway) and Brenda, and friends took turns keeping vigil and praying by his bedside.

Jill and Andrew survived their ordeals. Jill resumed her old occupations and activities, thankful for each moment that was given to her. Andrew was not so fortunate; his illness left him profoundly and permanently disabled. Then, after a long battle with breast cancer, Brenda died, leaving Harold alone to care for Andrew and his two older brothers.

Jill recalls the many ways that Harold, who still lives in the same duplex up the street from her parents' house, poured his life into his son's care. He carried his son up and down the stairs of their house. He sang Andrew's favorite song, "Jesus Loves Me," hundreds of times. He read stories, soothing Andrew with the reassuring sound of his voice.

The years passed, and Harold became physically unable to lift his son every day, so another family helped care for Andrew. He now lives with his special education teacher, and sometimes comes back to his old home for a visit. We occasionally see them together at church, as Harold pushes Andrew's wheelchair to the front of the nave so that he can receive Holy Communion.

As Andrew grew up, Jill married and had children of her own. When her fourth child and only son, Anatoli, was diagnosed with moderate autism, she posted a request on the church bulletin board for volunteers to help with Anatoli's home therapy program. Harold, who had retired after many years of teaching, called her up and offered to help.

Once a week, Anatoli visits Harold, who patiently and faithfully helps him to progress from a limited vocabulary and attention span to an ability to work with sounds, words, letters, and patterns for almost two hours at a stretch. During each visit together, Harold and Anatoli walk to the mailbox and back, and Anatoli loves to run up and down Andrew's wheelchair ramp on the front porch. Harold and Anatoli enjoy one another's company.

Harold is a quiet man who leads a quiet life. His living room is furnished sparely with an old sofa and a small entertainment center, on which sits a television and a few books and family photos. He doesn't own a computer. He attends church, visits his son, goes to appointments, checks his mail. There is, in fact, nothing outwardly remarkable about him or the life he leads.

But Jill knows better. She marvels at Harold's generosity and hopes that he feels blessed every time he notices that he has helped Anatoli acquire a new skill or learn a new lesson. How wonderful it would be if there were more Harolds willing to give their time and love to children who need them. For years, Jill knew Harold as Andrew's loving, faithful father. Now, she says, he is also Anatoli's angel.

A FEW YEARS AGO, A GROUP OF ST. JOHN'S WOMEN GATHERED at the Moose Lick, a comfortably rustic bed and breakfast, for a weekend getaway and spiritual retreat. On Saturday night, we relaxed on overstuffed sofas, and our talk turned to the challenges and joys of raising children.

The conversational ball bounced back and forth for awhile and Elise, a young mother, said with a trace of frustration in her voice, "I was born in the community and I grew up in it. I've lived my whole life surrounded by the church, our priests, my family and my friends. Sometimes I'm afraid my life has been *way* too sheltered."

Her honest expression of a point of view that is likely shared by other young adults who have never said it aloud, sparked a lot of comment, some in agreement with Elise's sentiment, some in disagreement. Finally, Eloise, Mara's grandmother and a strong woman who has fought her share of life's battles, spoke up and challenged us with a pointed question. "What's *wrong* with being sheltered?" she asked. "It meets *my* needs."

Thinking later about this lively discussion, I wondered why some people insist that "sheltering" children is a bad idea. What does that word mean, anyway? The dictionary says that *shelter* is derived from "shield troop," literally a body of men protected by interlocked shields. A shelter covers and protects from danger or the elements. Our Sunday school teachers taught us that Adam and Eve were sheltered in the Garden, that Noah and his family took refuge in the ark, and that Moses was covered by God's own hand. Churches have always been places of refuge, and God Himself is called in scripture a "fortress."

(Remember when I said that Barbara Dunaway modeled her vision of the St. John's community's Big House on L'Abri, the community founded by Dr. Francis and Edith Schaeffer in Switzerland? Interestingly, *l'abri* is a French word that means *shelter.* The L'Abri website says that the Schaeffers founded their community as a place where people could find practical demonstrations of Christian care and a shelter from the pressures of a relentlessly secular culture.)

Churches shelter the suffering, the sick and dying, the homeless, and all who are spiritually and emotionally needy. Strangers are welcomed and cared for. Parents bring their children to the font for baptism, we provide them with godparents who promise to pray for them and watch over their spiritual formation, and we make sure that they regularly receive Holy Communion, a powerful protector of soul and body. No one would argue that these are not good things.

Why, then, do we feel cautious about guarding our children too closely? This concern often arises when parents consider a Christian school for their children, and it has been addressed by our spiritual overseer, Bishop Joseph, whose commitment to Christian schools, along with his love for children, is obvious and great. "When we say *school*," he writes, "we don't mean budgets and buildings. We mean to build a *family*, planting seeds of faith and providing a clean environment for innocent children."

St. John's Orthodox Christian School was founded by parents "to provide an excellent academic education within the safe, nurturing environment of the St. John Cathedral community." When Bill and I decided to move the family from our Anchorage neighborhood to Monastery Drive in Eagle River, an important motivation was the desire to enroll our youngest son in the community's small school. We loved the fact that the Orthodox faith we chose to embrace would be reinforced every day in Travis's classroom.

Compared to Eagle River's public schools and many of its private ones, St. John's is small—small budget, small staff, small classes. But it is big in love for its students, the dedication of its teachers, and the commitment of its parents. It offers our church community and the greater community of Eagle River good things that are obviously in demand—about one-half of the school's families are not members of St. John's Church.

Many St. John's adults attended St. John's School and now have children of their own there. Still, participation of parish families in the school is not monolithic. Families are free to choose from a number of options: home school; public schools, both regular and charter; and other private schools in our area.

Some parents, here and in other church communities, knowing that Christians are to be "salt and light" in the world, believe that isolating our children in a small, fairly homogeneous school is not, in the long run, the right thing to do. But Fr. Marc, a firm advocate of Christian schools, likes to remind us of a popular trend in education, the foreign language "immersion programs," which often have long waiting lists for admission. Why not let our children learn in an atmosphere of "Christian immersion," he asks, where the lessons of reading and writing are integrated within an Orthodox view of God's creation?

It occurs to me that the objection to "Christian immersion" springs from the fear of rearing our children in a kind of religious "hothouse," an image that suggests rows of pampered, delicate plants that will shrivel and die if transplanted to a tougher environment. Sister Magdalen, an Orthodox nun and Christian school advocate, responded to this fear. "An Orthodox [or any Christian] school should be looked upon as a *greenhouse* for the cultivation of young and sensitive plants," she said. "They should grow here in preparation for later planting in the garden."

Looking back at Matthew 18, I see that Jesus took the disciples' question about who is greatest in the kingdom as an opportunity to issue a serious warning to the Church's leaders about their treatment of the "little ones," the innocent and childlike. His language could not have been much stronger. It turns out that the one who ignores or offends these little ones would be better off "if a millstone were hung around his neck, and he were drowned in the depth of the sea" (Matthew 18:6).

In their commentary on this verse, the editors of the *Orthodox Study Bible* point out that Jesus identified children as models of true disciples because they possess the spiritual attitudes necessary to enter the Kingdom—humility, dependence, lowliness, and simplicity. "Whoever receives one little child like this in My name receives Me," Jesus said. The little school in the St. John's community takes His words very seriously.

Only if you are childlike may you enter the kingdom of heaven. God's kingdom will have more "children" than bishops, priests, philosophers, politicians and so-called leaders of this world.

—METROPOLITAN (ARCHBISHOP) PHILIP SALIBA

COME TAKE LIGHT

MAY

FEAST OF THE RESURRECTION

*Christ is risen from the dead, trampling down death by death, and upon
those in the tombs bestowing life!*

—TROPARION OF THE FEAST

ON HOLY FRIDAY MORNING, WE WAKE TO SEE FAT SNOW-
flakes swirling from the sky to the muddy ground, and we cross our
fingers and say, "It won't stick. It's 40°, way too warm for it to stick."

But it does stick, and by the time the last flake has touched down,
like a tiny jumper wrapped in a billowy white chute, the neighborhood is covered by a blanket two feet thick. The really interesting
thing about this particular snowfall is not that it is happening in early
May, but that Easter this year is also happening in early May, and we
had been very sure that it would be the first snow-free Easter in recent
memory. But it was not to be, and we get out the snow shovels that
were prematurely put away, lamenting once again that Easter finery in

Alaska is more likely to feature snow boots and parkas than peep-toe pumps and gauzy spring frocks.

Pascha (Easter) is the Christian "Feast of Feasts." Fr. Marc says that every time he looks back on Holy Week, the days between Lent and Pascha that start with Lazarus Saturday and end with Holy Saturday, he is always amazed that we made it through all of the week's twenty-seven services. By the time we get to Holy Friday, he says, it feels as if we have left the world and are living in a different place, where we move to the Church's rhythm, not to the clock's.

On Holy Friday, the austerity of Lent and Holy Week finally begins to recede, and, even in the solemn scriptures and hymns about Jesus' crucifixion and death, we sense a current of joy. Because we know, even if Pilate and the Pharisees do not, that Resurrection is just ahead.

In the Gospel reading for Holy Friday, St. John says that two Pharisees, Joseph of Arimathea and Nicodemus, took charge of Jesus' body and that they "came, bringing a mixture of myrrh and aloes, about a hundred pounds. Then they took the body of Jesus, and bound it in strips of linen with the spices, as the custom of the Jews is to bury."

For several years now, my friend Sally and I have met on the afternoon of Holy Friday to decorate the *epitaphion*, the wooden platform on which a corpse or a coffin is placed, better known to us as the *bier*. Sally and I have no spices, but we do have bunches of dark green ruffled fern, bouquets of pale pink sweetheart roses, sturdy little pink and white carnations, and clouds of baby's breath, all waiting in pots beside the undecorated bier.

For the next two hours, we arrange and fasten the flowers into a lavish frame around the edge of the bier, in preparation for that evening, when the large crucifix will be removed from the front of the nave and the bier will be put in its place. Then Fr. Marc will arrange upon the bier the embroidered cloth icon of Christ's burial. Finally, on top of the cloth, he will lay the large Gospel book that represents Jesus, the Word. Sally and I love our job, and every year we remember the two Marys and Salome, the faithful myrrhbearing women who brought spices to Jesus' tomb to anoint His body, and we feel close to them.

Sally has a special reason for celebrating the Resurrection this year. Her mother, Mary Margaret, passed away last fall and is buried in the St. John's cemetery. Magi (pronounced "Maggie"), as everyone called her, was a tiny Texas gal for whom the word *spunky* was invented. In 1960 she decided to spread her wings and fly off to a teaching job in Anchorage. With her father, young son, and two Chihuahuas for company, she drove up the Alcan Highway, settled into a trailer in the Mountain View neighborhood, and taught Spanish to junior high schoolers.

During summer vacations, she went off adventuring, cooking at a fishing lodge on the Kenai River (where she once chased a bear out of the kitchen), cooking aboard the *Gypsy Queen,* a tour boat on Prince William Sound, and bartending on the scenic tracks of the Alaska Railroad.

Sally followed her mom to Alaska and discovered the Orthodox Church and the St. John's community. Magi, a long-time Episcopalian, attended St. John's with Sally and received chrismation at age 76, on the same day her great-grandson was baptized. On Pascha afternoon, Sally will take one or two flowers from the bier and lay them on her mother's grave.

Holy Saturday is a busy day for everybody in the community. Between morning and evening services, we color boiled eggs and fill our Easter baskets with the meat and cheese and butter we will serve as we "break the fast" on Sunday morning. Khouria[2] Betsy and her helpers decorate the social hall and prepare the lamb and chicken and steak kebabs that will be grilled and served at tomorrow's celebration. For three hours on Pascha afternoon, we will feast and sing and dance and laugh, as if at a great family reunion, where every year we renew ties of kinship by celebrating together the Resurrection of our Lord.

I'm in my kitchen, stirring batter for the coconut cake I will take to tomorrow's feast and thinking of the moist, yellow layer cakes with white meringue frosting that my Aunt Alice baked every Easter. She cracked a coconut and grated it by hand, then tinted the flakes green and sprinkled them on the white frosting. On top of the coconut "grass" she scattered colored jelly bean "eggs."

Each Orthodox national group loves its own celebration foods. The Greeks serve roasted lamb and *tsoureki paschalino*, a sweet dessert bread. The Arabs also enjoy lamb, along with *bahklava* and *kunafah*, sinfully sweet desserts. The Russians must have *kulich*, a tall, cylindrical yeast cake filled with dried fruit, spread with *paskha*, a pyramid-shaped sweet cheese mold, also stuffed with dried fruit. My neighbor Debbie molds her paskha into the shape of a lamb.

For our family breakfast after the Paschal Liturgy, my daughter-in-law, Anna, will bring kulich and paskha, in honor of her Russian grandmother, along with *nelisniky*, meat-filled crepes in mushroom gravy, a traditional dish made by her Ukrainian grandmother. And I, with at least some of my roots still firmly planted in the American South, will serve ham and cheesy grits.

---

2   In the Antiochian Church, *Khouria* is a customary title of respect for a priest's wife.

Through my kitchen window, I see Debbie's husband Dwight rumbling out of his driveway in the cab of his front-end loader. By day, Dwight is a compassionate and intelligent psychiatrist who cares for Alaska's prison inmates. Evenings and weekends, he relaxes behind the controls of his big rig and moves dirt, rocks, and even, on one occasion, a chicken coop. Yesterday's snowfall is dense and mushy this morning, so maybe he is headed to clear it from the church parking lot.

Bill goes out to chat with Al, who has dropped by to check on the boat parked in our driveway. Last summer, the two of them went in together to buy a fishing boat, and Al is itching to get it on the water. He grew up in Detroit, on Lake St. Clair, served on a U.S. Naval destroyer, and is one of our intrepid Kasilof River fishing captains. (There will be more about Kasilof later.)

Al's scarred, deeply seamed face reveals who he is—a man who has seen good times and hard times, happiness and despair, and continues, like the rest of us, to struggle against the arrows of the enemy. He is upfront about his background: He comes, he says, from a dysfunctional family of alcoholics, a family in which he recalls little love and even less discipline. He "grew up like a wild weed" and, once grown, embarked on a hedonistic and self-destructive life. For a long time, he never looked back. But of all the events in his life, none has remained as powerful in his memory as the night he was visited by a "being of light."

Al's story begins in 1975, when his brother Phil received a visit from two friends who showed up on a Harley-Davidson. Chris and his sister, Hope, invited Phil to go with them to Grace Haven Farm in Finley, Ohio, where they planned to attend talks given by Fr. Peter Gillquist, one of the seven men I mentioned earlier who were then finding their way to Orthodoxy. Phil went with them, and when he came back, Al saw that he acted differently, that he *was* different, not his old self at all.

Saturday came, and Al decided to spend the weekend doing what he enjoyed: drinking. Phil had always liked to spend his weekends the same way, so Al called him up and invited him to go along. By Sunday morning, the two of them had been kicked out of two bars, and Al suggested that they go to Uncle Fritz's, a favorite place. To his amazement, Phil said no, he was not going. Al looked his brother in the eye and "saw something I had never seen in the thirty years I had known him." He suspected that Phil's change of heart had something to do with God and with his experience at the farm in Ohio. Right then, Al says, he had the first inkling that maybe there really was a God, if He was able to make Phil turn down a drink and go home.

Soon, Phil accepted Chris's latest invitation, to go up to Alaska and check out the Big House at Eagle River, a community of Christians that Chris and his sister had learned of and in which they intended to live. When Phil left, he gave Al a simple cross and told him, "I don't want you to wear this until you know what it means." The cross meant absolutely nothing to Al, but he thumbtacked it to the wall beside his bed and resumed his party lifestyle.

That lifestyle eventually included traffic tickets, DUIs, and, occasionally, jail time. His out-of-control drinking had driven away his friends, his parents no longer wanted him around, and he was barred from entering his younger brother's home. He was "a functioning alcoholic, a big-time loser." He thought about suicide, but realized that he did not have the "courage" to do it. He was just past thirty years old, and the lifestyle was no longer a source of amusement and pleasure. It was a dead end and he could not find the way out.

As he got into bed one night, still thinking about how suicide would make his troubles go away, he remembered the look in Phil's eyes and how his brother had seemed to be changed. Al didn't know if God was inclined to listen to him, or if He even existed, but he got on his knees and began talking.

"I'm screwed up," he said. "I know I'm screwed up and I don't want to live anymore. I don't believe in you, I don't even believe you're there. But if you can help me, like you helped my brother, I'm asking you to."

He got into bed and whether he slept or not, he can't say. He does know that sometime during that troubled night, he felt a pressure on his chest, and he sensed that it came from the hand of a "being of light" that stood beside his bed. He tried and felt unable to move, then finally gave up the struggle. It was then that he felt all the dark, painful things being drawn out of his life, to be replaced by an awareness of light, a feeling that every cell of his body was filled with happiness. He was so full of light and joy that he wanted nothing more than to simply lie there and experience that feeling. Eventually, he went back to sleep.

The next morning he woke, and was immediately conscious that there was a God, that he had been in contact with Him, and that the experience was wonderful. He had to tell somebody about it. So he called his brother Daryl. Daryl listened to his story and laughed at him.

Next he talked to Dale, a guy he worked with who was known to be religious. Dale listened to the story, put his hand on Al's shoulder and said, "Al, you certainly are a troubled man. But God does not do that kind of thing. What you experienced was a vivid dream. I can give you some books that will help you." Dale was a Jehovah's Witness, and his books didn't help Al very much.

There was another guy at work, Bob, who was also known to be religious in the charismatic tradition of evangelicals. Bob and Al never got along, and avoided being assigned to the same job. One day, they could not escape working together, and their first call was at a church. Al decided to tell Bob his story. Bob got excited. He said, "Al, you said a sincere prayer and God answered it in a miraculous way. Now it's up to you to deal with it."

"What do I do?" Al asked.

Bob told him everything he knew about God. The only thing he was unsure of was the day Jesus planned to come back to earth. Al, he said, needed to pray and ask Jesus to come into his heart, so that he would be saved and become His child. Bob urged him to do it right then, but Al decided he would do it later. That night he went to a place that always made him feel good—a marina, where the water lapped gently against the rocks and glowed in the reflection of city lights. He knelt and said the sinner's prayer, and right away felt calm and clean for the first time in his life.

Next morning he told Bob he had said the prayer. Bob invited him to church. Al had never been to church and was uncomfortable with the idea but, figuring that God had brought him this far, he decided to go. It was a little Pentecostal church, with lots of kids and only a couple of adults. A young man led them in singing the song about God telling Noah to "build me an arky, arky," and Al tried to join in and make the animal motions like the kids were doing.

When the song was over, he started for the door, disappointed by this strange church service, but he felt a hand on his shoulder and Bob said, "Al, if you can get through that, then you're definitely going to make it." It turned out the men had been having prayer meeting in another room while the children met in the sanctuary.

Al got baptized a week later and kept on going to church. He was prayed over and urged to speak in tongues, but it never happened. He prayed, fasted, and went on weekly "door knockings" to invite folks to church. He was trying, as best he knew how, to seek God's will for his life.

He decided to go to Alaska and check out what was happening there. On his first night at the Big House, he was "blown away" by the teaching he heard. When Al makes up his mind about something, he doesn't let the grass grow under his feet. He quit his job, sold his house, and found his place in the community in Eagle River.

Five years later, he married Rosalie and started a family that would eventually include three daughters. He described himself as a "blessed man." Once, before going to Alaska, he was asked to fill out a questionnaire on the subject of spiritual gifts. He could not think of any that he had. Now, he says, he has received two gifts—his encounter with God and his marriage to Rosalie. Al always makes me laugh, but, at the same time, he is one of those people whose funny observations often include great insight.

After thirty years as an Orthodox Christian, Al thinks about that night in his bed and still does not know what, or whom, he saw. He only knows that his life was transformed by the experience, and that the value of this knowledge is beyond price. Since that night he has, like the rest of us, backslid and sinned, for sure. But he is still here, still in the race, headed toward the Light.

COME TAKE LIGHT FROM THE LIGHT THAT IS NEVER OVERTAKEN. Come glorify Jesus whom we praise and magnify. It is almost five o'clock on Pascha morning, and holding tightly to Bill's arm, I walk near the front of a long procession line that is moving toward the doors of the closed, dark cathedral. The church bell tolls and, in the cold stillness before dawn, the sound seems to echo from the nearby mountains. I turn, and the scene behind me looks like a *National Geographic* photo, taken, perhaps, in some small, Slavic village. Three hundred people, well bundled against the cold, hold lighted candles and step carefully through the slushy snow, singing together the Hymn of Light. In this ritual procession, the closed, dark church is an icon of Jesus' tomb, and we are going there to commemorate the discovery by His disciples that He is no longer there, but is risen.

We enter the warm cathedral as every light is snapped on, and we feel as if we have crossed a threshold between winter and springtime. Every year, after the evening liturgy of Holy Saturday, Judi and her helpers stay behind to arrange the flowers, garlands, banners, and baskets of greenery, transforming the nave into a secret garden that will remain in place until the Feast of Ascension, forty days from now. Inside the cathedral, everything is bright and fragrant, and the nave rings with the singing of Paschal Matins: *This is the day which the Lord has made! Let us rejoice and be glad in it!*

Judi tells me there is a woman—not a St. John's parishioner—who visits the cathedral each Paschal season to sit in the nave and admire its beauty. I can understand this. From Pascha to Ascension, I love finding excuses to slip into the church and smell the incense and flowers, and to listen as the empty nave seems to echo with the censer bells and the joyous Paschal greeting: *Christ is risen!*

Rosalie prayed that she would "make it to Pascha" (which means *passage*), and she did. Thin and frail, she nevertheless celebrated with us at the Feast. In that world outside of time, the Church's commemoration of Holy Week and its celebration of the Resurrection, I pray that

70

she, and all of us, glimpsed a way of living not marked, like man's life, by the tick of a clock, but rather like that of the angels—by the never-ending hymns of praise.

> *For today as from a bridal chamber, Christ has shone forth from the tomb, and filled the women with joy, saying: Proclaim the glad tidings to the apostles!*
>
> —PASCHAL MATINS

PRACTICAL SISTERS
AND GIVERS OF LOVE

JUNE

FEAST OF ASCENSION

You have ascended in glory, Christ our God, You have made glad the disciples by the promise of the Holy Spirit; through this blessing You have truly assured them that You are the Son of God, the Redeemer of the world.

—TROPARION OF THE FEAST

IT IS JUNE NOW AND THE LONG WINTER IS A FADED MEMORY, swept away by a warm wind that smells like lilacs and cut grass and freshly turned earth. The sun has done a complete about-face, and we confound our Lower Forty-eight friends and relatives by our ability to sleep in the "white nights" of the Arctic. When people ask me how we bear the short winter days, I always remind them that Alaska gets just as much daylight as any other place—only ours is portioned out to us differently.

It is a bright and breezy summer morning, and I am headed to Barbara's for tea with the Wednesday morning ladies' reading group. Barbara and Fr. Harold live in the Maranatha House, the one that faces the cathedral across the wide lawn and is just a few steps away from the Big House. Their new deck, with its comfy cushioned chairs and pots of blooming flowers, will be a perfect spot for tea and lunch.

A sunny day in our neighborhood brings everyone outdoors, and many of us wind up gathering somewhere on the church lawn, which is a lot like a village green, without the livestock. A group of kids has a baseball game going on one end, while the teenagers working in the St. John's Summer Youth Corps weed and rake flowerbeds at another.

In front of the Big House, our neighbor and mechanical trouble-shooter, Bob, has opened the well hole for repairs, and I peek over the edge, hoping to get a look at the railroad tanker car that was buried there many years ago to store water. But all I see is the top of Bob's head; he shouts hello and assures me that the tanker is right there beneath his feet.

I join the group of ladies on the deck and we chat for awhile, passing around sandwiches and fruit. We find a spot to settle with our tea and lemonade and listen as Eloise, in her soft, precise voice, describes her recent photo safari to Kenya and Tanzania. She made the trip on her eightieth birthday, in memory of her dad, who dreamed of going to Africa but never made it. Eloise is a petite lady who looks *much* younger than her years. She is self-possessed and wise, and she always laughs when I tell her, as I often do, that she is one of my favorite role models.

Then Phebe, Barbara's sister, introduces the book the ladies will read this summer. It is *Mayflower,* a new book that aims to tell the real story of the Pilgrims and the Indians. Phebe says she was brought up to regard the Pilgrims as American saints, but after reading this book, she realized they were not saints at all. They were, in fact, "a little twisted." Well, that gets *my* attention, and I decide to pick up a copy and join the ladies' group for the summer.

The talk about Pilgrims and Indians reminds us of the concert at the Native Heritage Center last week. Steven and his band, Medicine Dream, were on stage, and a big group from St. John's was on hand to enjoy their music. Steven is a passionate and gifted musician, a vocalist and percussionist, who performs, alone and in groups, all over the country. He is also an Orthodox Christian and lends his considerable gifts to the St. John's choir.

You only have to look at Steven to know his ethnic heritage. His face might have been carved from desert stone, and straight, black hair streams down his back. He identifies himself as Mescalero Apache and Yaqui/Upper Tanana Athabascan. On stage, dressed in leather and beads, feathers woven into his hair, he looks like he belongs on a horse, racing toward the sun.

Medicine Dream's music is a "Native pop-rock fusion," a blend of ancient tribal chants and modern rock riffs. It throbs with drumbeats and sizzles with rattling, tinkling instruments, occasionally featuring the lonely cry of a Native flute. Most every song includes haunting interludes of *"way-hey-hey-ya-yo-way-hey"* chant, and the effect is hypnotic and powerful.

Back on the deck, Gwen is saying that the Indians surely endured a lot of misery at the hands of white people and she is glad to see them rediscovering their culture. Barbara replies, a little tartly I think, that she hopes while rediscovering it, they do not separate themselves from the culture of the rest of the country.

Oh no, Gwen disagrees, that's not what they are trying to do at all. They only want to reconnect with their own history.

I smile and make myself more comfortable in my chair. A little controversy is brewing along with the tea.

Well, Barbara shrugs, maybe so.

Phebe announces that Steven suggested we put on an Indian pow-wow right here on Monastery Drive. The Indians, he says, will supply the costumes, drums, and dancing—all we have to bring is the food and drink.

No, Eloise says firmly, that isn't a good idea. An Indian powwow should be held on Indian land.

Barbara reminds her that at the concert the other night, Medicine Dream announced an upcoming powwow to be celebrated at a downtown city park. What do we think about that?

Eloise considers it and says yes, downtown Anchorage is a fine place for such a function.

Now that we've settled that, the conversation flows in other directions, and the afternoon drifts pleasantly away.

WALKING HOME FROM THE LADIES' TEA, I WAVE AT TISHA, A tall former ballerina who moved from California to Alaska to get married and settle in the community. She sits on her front porch, soaking up the sun, lulled by the drowsy hum of bees. Her husband Joe is a beekeeper, and one of his hives lives on their front porch.

Last summer, the front porch hive attracted a young black bear who coveted the "brood," the hatchling bees, inside it. (Forget Winnie the Pooh and his "hunny pot." Joe informs me that bears are not interested in honey; it only gets in their way.) It was around 5:00 A.M. when the bear stepped boldly onto the wooden porch and managed to get the hive turned over, creating a racket that gave neighbor Judi, out to get her morning paper, quite a turn.

The disappointed bear ran away, but Joe knew the intrepid creature would not be able to resist coming back for another try at those grubs, so he drove nails through a board and fastened it to his porch rail. Tisha says she loves to watch the bees come and go, each of them knowing exactly what he was put on this earth to do and doing his best to accomplish it, without complaint or question. She says she learns a lot from those bees.

Farther down the street, I meet an elderly couple, holding hands, moving slowly. Fr. Jack and Esther are out for their afternoon stroll. One of the band of seven who searched for the New Testament Church and found Orthodoxy, Fr. Jack is a PhD and former statistics professor. He left a teaching job at Penn State to join the staff of Campus Crusade for Christ and, at the height of the sixties' agitation, he was sent to evangelize the students at the University of California at Berkeley. From *Right On,* the newspaper produced by the World Liberation Front (his Berkeley organization of campus Christians), to his editorial oversight of the recently published *Orthodox Study Bible,* Fr. Jack has been writing and teaching for forty years.[3]

On his first day at Berkeley, he witnessed a regular event which he remembers as "Noon Riot." Each day at noon, someone climbed the steps of Sproul Hall and introduced a speaker. The speaker's job was to inflame the crowd with counterculture rhetoric, after which a band of students, radicals, and street people began an "impromptu" march.

---

3   Fr. Jack Sparks reposed in the Lord on Feb. 8, 2010, while this book was in production. Memory eternal!

The march turned into a melee, during which the participants yelled, broke windows, and started fires in trash cans. Eventually, the riot was broken up and the group dispersed, only to show up the next day and repeat the performance. Fr. Jack still chuckles when he remembers those days.

The three of us chat for a minute or two, then part ways.

Now I am passing Al's place, and I notice the newly planted flowerbeds next to the driveway near the road. I remember another warm summer afternoon when his wife Rosalie, her face flushed and her hands dirty, lugged the big rocks to outline each of those beds. Like small tenders around the mother ship, her daughters brought the trays of yellow marigolds and blue petunias and helped Rosalie plant them. And I remember the song of Medicine Dream: *Though you are gone, we remember you. Though you are not here, we pray for you.*

On my very first Easter morning at St. John's, I saw Rosalie in the narthex after Liturgy, surrounded by friends who were invited to her house for breakfast. "Come on over," I heard her tell them. "I'll start frying the bacon." I looked on wistfully and wished that I could be among those lucky ones invited to Rosalie's house for breakfast. Somehow I knew, without yet knowing her, that her home was a good, warm place to be.

Not long after, we too were lucky enough to be invited to Rosalie's house. Al always said that she had an "open door" attitude, and she did. Everyone felt welcomed at her table, and once you were *in*, you stayed in. Rosalie's house was one of those rare places where you could drop by anytime, and feel immediately comfortable and at home.

Raised in a close-knit farming family, Rosalie was a Bible-believing, independent Protestant whose determination to follow the will of God led her from the wheat fields of Kansas to the mission field in the jungle of Ecuador. Her college roommate, Maye, invited her to visit the St. John's church and community; she came and, after living here and thinking it over for a year, chose to embrace the Orthodox faith and make her home with the people in Eagle River.

Rosalie and Al were not kids when they married, so they started a family right away. Their girls, Mary Ruth, Rebecca, and Martha, are famous around here for their sisterly cohesion and for the spark of fun they strike as soon as they get to the party. It was they who mischievously named their dad's boating excursions "Al's Torture Charters."

Al and Rosalie invited our family to join them on the Kasilof River, where they introduced us to "setnetting," a type of subsistence fishing which requires a large net to be anchored near the shoreline at low tide. This is followed by hours spent around a campfire, laughing and talking, until the tide comes in and the net is, one hopes, filled with trapped salmon. When the tide was at its highest, we all piled into Al's truck and careened through the wet sand to check the net. It was lots of fun.

Later, setnetting was replaced by dipnetting and, again, Al and Rosalie taught us how to do it. And again, it was fun because Rosalie knew how to make even a rainy, dismal campsite on the beach into a happy, cozy place.

It was on a hot summer afternoon, just after we had all been to a local air show together, that Rosalie told us about her breast cancer. She was a bit vague, but we understood that it was fairly advanced, and that she would be receiving several different treatments.

Most people are familiar with what follows a cancer diagnosis—the hopefulness before the treatment begins, the coping with the side effects, the anguish when the results are not what was hoped and prayed for.

By the following Christmas, her cancer was advancing, and Rosalie and Al considered moving the family to Kansas, to be near her strong extended family. But Rosalie decided against going back to Kansas. When she chose to turn to Orthodoxy, she knew that meant, in a sense, turning from her past life. It did not mean renouncing all the beliefs of her good Protestant forebears, but rather going, in C. S. Lewis's words, "further up, further in." The Orthodox Church became her home, and the people of St. John's were her family. In the St. John's community, she had found her place.

Rosalie's prayer was answered, and she did "make it to Pascha." In fact, she lived to celebrate the Feast of Ascension, which follows forty days after Pascha and marks the risen Christ's departure into heaven. I was at her house on a clear June morning when she died, friends and family at her side.

Barbara P., who oversees our cemetery, is a sturdy, capable lady who seems never to speak without first pausing to organize her thoughts. When she speaks, her words are sensible and well chosen. Death, she says, mobilizes the St. John's community. Everyone can find a job to do: cooking and cleaning for the family; digging the grave; building the coffin; planning the funeral service; rehearsing the music; writing the obituary; offering comfort. Barbara recalls Grammy Phyl's death, the first time she helped to prepare a friend's body for her funeral. "Nothing in my middle-class background prepared me for doing that. But it just seemed right to join in a practical act of love with my grieving sisters."

Before Rosalie's body was placed in the handmade wooden coffin, she was carefully washed and anointed and dressed by her practical and loving sisters, Lori, JoAnn, and Theresa. The evening of the day she died, in the same ritual that was repeated for Grammy Phyl and others, the community carried Rosalie's coffin to the cathedral.

Her funeral day was warm and bright, a perfect Alaska summer day, the breeze sweetened by purple and pink lilacs. Bells tinkled on the swinging censer, and clouds of incense drifted upward in the sun-filled cathedral. Rosalie was surrounded by her priests and deacons, her family and friends. I stood near her coffin and noticed the prayer rope in her hands, the tiny icon of St. John Maximovitch pinned to her dress.

I am squeamish about looking at a dead body. I try to excuse myself on the grounds of trauma at age fourteen, when I suddenly found myself beside my daddy's open casket, the first time I ever saw death. But that is not a very good excuse. Every human must come to terms with the sight of death, and everyone's first experience, I am sure, is frightening in some way.

But to Orthodox Christians, the human body, even after death, is an honorable, holy thing. Our bodies before death have been washed in baptism and anointed with the oil of chrism, have partaken of the body and blood of Christ in the Eucharist, were crowned in marriage, kissed the icons, stood in prayer, read the Scriptures—in short, have participated in the worship of God. True, the body will return to dust, but on the last day, in a miracle, it will be raised again.

Duke, our neighbor and a former funeral director, believes this is the reason the Orthodox funeral tradition is such a healthy one. Although no one is ever forced to gaze upon death, neither are we encouraged to hide from it. "The whole Orthodox funeral process," Duke says, "gives parents a chance to teach their children about dying and death in a way that creates respect and lessens their fear."

Duke is one of those versatile guys who seems to know some-thing about everything. He is lean and energetic, and his friendly face creases in a patient smile through all our nervous jokes and questions about his old line of work.

He says the hardest thing to deal with in Alaska was the great number of "immediate disposals" he had to arrange. This happens when a family or next of kin chooses a quick cremation or burial with no service, no obituary, no prayer or word of any kind. "People usually claim that money is the problem," he says, "but I always made it clear to people who came to me that money should never be the main issue."

The real reasons, he says, for so many "immediate disposals" in Alaska are our exceptionally transient population; our remote locations and the extra time it often takes for family members to get here; and a diminishing emphasis in general on any kind of spiritual life.

Duke is familiar with funerals in the Orthodox Native villages of bush Alaska—which often take place over several days—along with Orthodox funerals in the larger cities, all of which are a far cry from "immediate disposal."

When the funeral prayers for Rosalie were finished, it was time for each of us to walk past her coffin to say goodbye. I could hardly bear to watch as Rosalie's daughters looked, for the last time, at their mother's earthly face. Fr. Marc sprinkled her body with the holy water, then the coffin was sealed for one more procession, to the cemetery. The priests led, carrying icons and the censer. Deacons followed with the heavy crucifix and the large icon banner of the Resurrection of Christ. Friends carried Rosalie's coffin, and the rest of us followed while the church bell tolled once for each year of her life.

It is not far from the cathedral to the cemetery—just across the lawn and a short walk up Monastery. To the right of the road, screened by trees and overlooking a steep hill where children ride their sleds in winter, the small cemetery is dotted with wooden crosses and granite headstones. Gordon and his crew dug the new grave by hand, and a pot full of dirt rested on a table beside it.

More prayers were said, and the coffin was lowered into the ground, the ropes slithering through the men's hands and pulled out. "Ashes to ashes, dust to dust . . ." Fr. Marc said, and tipped the hot censer over the grave, releasing a little shower of ash. He picked up a handful of dirt and let it fall onto the coffin, tracing the sign of the cross. The rest of us walked past the open grave, and our handfuls of dirt fell with little thudding noises onto the wood.

On Rosalie's gravestone are the words, "Giver of Love," and there could be no better description. When I think of her, she is always in motion—hot-mopping and grooming the small ice rink she and Al made in their back yard where the neighborhood kids played hockey; canning and smoking the red salmon she helped pull from the Kasilof River; pressing the seal into the top of the *prosphora,* the Eucharist bread she baked; gathering friends together at her house to sing the special hymn, the *akathist,* to her beloved St. John Maximovitch. Death slowed her, but I can't believe that it stopped her, not as long as God's love embraces her. When we sing the final hymn of the funeral service, "Memory Eternal," we are praying that God will keep her in His everlasting love.

Orthodox funerals are the antithesis of "immediate disposal" because, to us, death is not "the end." Rosalie and the others are not left alone in the peaceful cemetery. They are remembered with prayers on anniversaries of their passing, on the Saturday of Souls a week before Lent, and with an Easter afternoon gathering of the parish at the cemetery, where we pray and sing hymns about resurrection.

Barbara P. taught us how to make *koliva,* or memorial wheat, the traditional dish of boiled wheat, nuts, fruit, and honey that is served on occasions when we remember our departed loved ones. As we eat it, we remember Jesus' words from John 12:24: "Most assuredly, I say to you, unless a grain of wheat falls into the ground and dies, it remains alone; but if it dies, it produces much grain." And we are reassured that, like seeds, the bodies of the departed, including my dear friend Rosalie, are only hidden in the ground, waiting to rise again in the springtime of the resurrection.

> *O relatives and close ones of the dead! Do for them what is needful for them and within your power. Use your money not for outward adornment of the coffin and grave, but in order to help those in need. . . . Show mercy to the dead, take care of their souls. Before us all stands the same path, and how we shall then wish that we would be remembered in prayer! Let us therefore be ourselves merciful to the dead.*
>
> —St. John Maximovitch of Shanghai
> and San Francisco

THE PORTABLE COMMUNITY

JULY

FEAST OF PENTECOST

Blessed are You, O Christ our God, who showed the fishermen to be most
wise by sending them the Holy Spirit, and used them to draw the whole
world into Your net. O You who love all men, glory to You.

—TROPARION OF THE FEAST

THE SAINTS, AND MANY A COUNSELOR AND THERAPIST AS
well, advise us to live in the present, neither fretting over what is past
nor worrying about what is yet to come. It's hard to follow that advice
when we seem to spend each minute either preparing for the next
one or regretting whatever we did in the last one. But summertime
in Alaska—so brief, so bright, so intense—is a good time to work on
living in the moment.

It is a cool, overcast July day here on the beach. The Feast of
Pentecost has come and gone, and a whole bunch of St. John's neighbors have made our yearly pilgrimage to the Kenai Peninsula south
of Anchorage. On the windy southern shore of Cook Inlet, we have
set up a temporary community of tents and RVs and are here to catch

salmon, hopefully lots of them, as many (within our legal limit, of course) as we can gather into our nets.

The state of Alaska, on certain rivers and at certain times, allows its residents to harvest the salmon run with long-handled dipnets. We are camped near the mouth of the Kasilof River, where it empties into the ocean waters of Cook Inlet. Captain Al pilots his small boat up and down the mouth of the river while four crew members drag nets in the cold, silty water. When we feel a bump against the net, we haul it up, dump the surprised fish into a cooler and stick the net right back into the water to wait for the next one. If we luck into a big run of salmon, we will fill our freezers for a year. If not—well, as Duke, another of our captains and also a philosopher, likes to say, "They call it fishin', not catchin'."

Everyone is out in the boats except Duke's wife, Lori, her children, and me. Lori is a nurse, so she knows how to take care of people. She also knows salmon and how to feed a crowd. Lori will use some of the fish next spring to prepare *Psari Plaki* for the dinner she helps serve to the whole community on the Feast of Annunciation. Rosalie taught Lori how to preserve salmon in cans, using her own jalapeño pepper recipe, and Lori, in turn, taught Theresa and me. For this trip, Lori has brought along a big pot of her Moose Barley Stew, and she is warming it over the fire. When the boats come back, with or without salmon, everyone will be hungry.

I am on the shore team this afternoon, and while I wait, I'm sitting on a slippery gray log which at first I call driftwood, until I decide that it probably did not wash ashore but was placed there by a previous camper for our convenience. No matter—it belongs there, and I am reminded of the huge piece of gnarled wood that I persuaded Bill to load into the truck and take home from a previous trip to the Kasilof.

It was so heavy that we could barely lift it, but I was determined to use it as a lawn ornament. We unloaded it at home, but a strange thing happened. The log gradually dried, then started to crumble and break apart, and it was no longer heavy. It was as if, removed from its accustomed environment, it could not maintain its old form.

Not unlike ourselves, I think. Like other immigrants, we who migrated to Alaska, transplanted from our original environments, are changed by our new surroundings and forced to adapt. And as so many of us St. John's converts chose to leave our original spiritual environment—whether Southern Baptist, Roman Catholic, or no church at all—we have sometimes been able to adapt, and sometimes we have just had to change.

In front of me is the ocean, flat and gray, the white, volcanic peaks of Mt. Iliamna and Mt. Redoubt outlined faintly in the distance. The beach is littered with whatever the tide has brought it—mostly mushy kelp and bits of shell. The air smells beachy, like salt and damp and rotting fish. Tall grasses wave nearby, reminding me of the big pots of leafy alder branches we brought into the church for Pentecost. Green is the color of Pentecost.

St. Luke says that just before the descent of the Holy Spirit, Christ's Mother, His apostles, and about a hundred other believers got together in the upper room in Jerusalem, where they prayed "with one accord" (all agreeing and no one dissenting). On the actual Day of Pentecost, when the wind blew through the whole house and the tongues of fire sat upon them, they were still "all with one accord in one place." So on the most basic theological level, which is the only level I am qualified to talk about, it seems that the Holy Spirit came upon them not only because of who they were, or where they were, or what they were saying, but because they were *united*. In the words of the *Orthodox Study*

Bible, "Their unity creates an environment in which the Holy Spirit will come."

The boats and their crews return, loaded with salmon. Because the fish were pulled from the salt water of Cook Inlet, before enduring the hardships of an upriver journey to the spawning grounds, they are fat and shiny, and their flesh is firm and red and very good to eat. Al reminds us of this every year, and he is right.

For the next hour or so, we work in an assembly line of intense, but usually calm, activity. Fish are pulled from the box and handed to cutters, who slice off the heads and scoop out the guts. Fish parts are tossed into the water and snatched by the circling, shrieking gulls. Other team members wash the gutted fish in the cold surf before plopping them into coolers of ice, which still others have prepared and brought to the beach. A particularly big catch might call for an emergency "ice run," and the designated team will hop into the nearest vehicle and head for the convenience stores on the highway. Once the catch is put on ice, the coolers are hauled back to the campsite and stowed under tarps.

A good catch puts a smile on everyone's face, and when the work is done, we can wash up, open a cold drink, and turn our attention to food. After Lori's moose stew is passed around and savored, Susie brings out a pie, warm from the oven in her RV, and coffee cups are filled. Bob stokes the campfire, which never goes completely out during our long weekend, and we pull our chairs around it for an evening of talk.

We watch as a long line of commercial fishing boats queues up in the inlet, waiting to enter the Kasilof, where they will unload their catch and get ready to go out again. The hum and throb of their engines keeps time with their twinkling lights, dancing in the wind like diamonds on a long, invisible chain.

Our young children play nearby in the sand, and our teenagers drift back and forth from the grownup circle to one of their own, waiting for more darkness so they can set off the fireworks they brought with them.

Our firelit circle never divides into smaller conversation groups. Throughout the evening, it stays unified and whole as we listen to our storytellers, Deacon Dan and Al, Jan and Bill. Theresa and Maye, the historians, reminisce about how we all came to be together in this place. MaryAnn remembers Rosalie, whose campsite was always our anchor and home base.

The desire of Christians, and of people in general, to gather in close community is nothing new, and we in Eagle River are certainly not unique. From the earliest Christians, of whom the Book of Acts says "all who believed were together and had all things in common"; to the rise of monasteries in the deserts and forests; to the New England Puritans with their vision of a "city set on a hill"; to the later utopians like the Oneida Colony; to the Shakers, whose rule of celibacy has reduced their number to one or two; to the Jesus movement of the 1960s and 70s; right up to the Amish of today—Christians have always desired to share more of their lives than just a couple of hours together on Sunday morning.

Back in 1974, at the height of the Jesus Movement and its embrace of community, Dave and Neta Jackson wrote *Living Together in a World Falling Apart*, in which they chronicled their own search for Christian community and reflected on the value of what they called *church-community*. It is interesting to read the story of their search in light of what was happening at that same time at the Big House in Eagle River, Alaska.

As they visited and observed a dozen church-communities, the authors identified their characteristics: a common life; sharing of money and possessions; a consciousness of the presence and power of the Holy Spirit; a witness for peace and nonviolence; and an emphasis on the teachings of Christ. Living in a church-community, they concluded, "provides a channel for the power of the Holy Spirit to minister to situations where 'free-lance' Christians flounder." It is a "strategy for faithfulness and wholeness."

But they saw one more thing by which a Christian community can be known: the love God's people show for one another. "This is the greatest similarity we saw in the communities we visited—God's people in active, loving relationships."

The young Big House community did not fit neatly into the Jacksons' pattern. The folks there lived a common life, insofar as that meant shared goals, dreams, and labor. (There was never "communal living"—living arrangements have always been creative but thoroughly conventional.) Their emphasis on the teachings of Christ dated back to the early days of Campus Crusade and its Four Spiritual Laws, which relied on the Gospels to communicate the plan of salvation. The young people went to Harold and Barbara Dunaway, hungry for scriptural teaching, and they stayed at Fern Street and Monastery Drive for that same reason.

In contrast to the Jacksons' ideas, the Big House was not a church, did not call itself one, and was wary of the whole idea of church. Church, and all that it entails, would come later. As for the notion of a "common purse," that requirement is the one most likely to get a church-community in trouble and is often followed quickly by the "cult" label. At no time (then or now) was anyone in the community expected to divest himself of worldly possessions and turn over the proceeds to anyone. Finally, unlike other communities whose aim was to witness to the Christian teachings on peace, sharing, and brotherhood, the group at the Big House did not come together to fight the ills of society. Though its individual members might be pacifists, environmentalists, or activists against racial injustice, the community has never identified itself with any particular social movement or cause.

The manifestation of the presence and power of the Holy Spirit in a church is often subjective; there is much agreement and some difference of opinion among Christians about how or even whether the Spirit's presence can be gauged. Therefore, being no kind of expert on the subject, I will simply say that in my view, one of the remarkable features of the St. John's community is its *evolution* through the years—from a hippie Bible study group that had no use for church, to a parish of the "one, holy, Catholic and Apostolic Church," with all the varied stops in between—and I would submit that it is difficult to argue that these changes were not inspired and directed by the Holy Spirit.

But the bottom line, as the Jacksons pointed out, is that any group of Christians (whether living together or scattered apart) must be mindful of the daily, practical, self-denying love that is required of us, the kind of love that Jesus commanded His followers to show when He said, "You shall love your neighbor as yourself." Barbara Dunaway expressed this commitment to *agape* early on in her Big House newsletter. The group there, she said, was trying in "practical relationships together . . . to know some of the reality of what Jesus meant when He prayed to the Father 'that they may be perfected in unity; that the world may know that Thou didst send Me.'"

Reading these words reminds me of Clyde, a tough old Wyoming cowboy who was baptized at St. John's and now rests in our cemetery. Here's how he described community: "To tell the truth, the most meaningful thing to me about this community is the people in it. It's the way I'm treated."

As always, I must add that although many of us have chosen to live close together near the church, other St. John's parishioners live elsewhere in Eagle River and Anchorage, so it is not mere physical location that binds us all together. The Holy Spirit did not descend on the apostles because they happened to be sitting together in the same room on the same street in the same city. It is the mutual assent to the basics of our faith—the basics that were hammered out with great effort and sometimes at great cost by the Church's councils—that is at the heart of Christian community.

It is an ironic twist in the St. John's community story that its first members were held together by a shared disillusionment with the established churches. Nevertheless, from the beginning, they believed that *together* they could move from agreement about what the Church *is not,* to discover the truth about what the Church *is.*

And this is the twist: The truth that was revealed to the community was the truth of Orthodox Christianity, the traditional, liturgical *Church.* In the church's archives, I found a letter written by Fr. Marc in 1986 as the community prepared to be received *en masse* into a strange and, to them, mysterious body. "How do we—how do I—face the many questions and difficulties that confuse and frighten me?" he wrote. *"By staying together to determine God's will."*

In *The Descent of the Holy Spirit,* Henri Nouwen's meditation on icons, he contemplates the fifteenth-century Russian icon of Pentecost and says that "a life in the Spirit is in essence a life in community."

Once we understand this, he adds, our concern shifts from questions about *my* spiritual life to the realization that "we can no longer separate the spiritual life from life in community, belonging to God from belonging to each other, and seeing Christ from seeing one another in Him."

The fire smolders and the breeze on the beach is chilly, but our portable community is snug and cozy. Each of us is reluctant to make the first move to get up and head to our tent or RV. But we do not yet have enough fish to provide a good catch to each family, so we must go out again tomorrow morning and put our nets in the water and see what will happen. Rain is in the forecast, so the next day's work is likely to be cold, damp, and maybe downright unpleasant. But it is made easier, as so many tasks are, because we will do it together.

The mystery of the Church consists in the very fact that together sinners become something different from what they are as individuals; this something different is the body of Christ.

—FR. JOHN MEYENDORFF

MYSTERY AND TRANSFORMATION

AUGUST

FEAST OF THE TRANSFIGURATION

*You were transfigured upon the mountain, O Christ our God, showing
Your disciples Your glory as far as they were able to bear it. At the prayers
of the Mother of God make Your everlasting light shine forth upon us sinners. O Giver of Light, glory to You.*

—TROPARION OF THE FEAST

EVERYONE KNOWS THAT THE INUIT HAVE A HUNDRED
different words for snow. Well, actually, I investigated this claim and
learned it is an urban legend—the Alaska Natives have no more words
for snow than do we English-speaking immigrants. But I also learned
that the Aleuts do have at least seven words for wind: *slatux*, to blow
hard; *slachxidaasaadagûlux*, a very strong storm; *ala ulix*, to go into the
sea; *asxi-lix*, to go against the wind; *qutaxt*, blowing up from land; *qag,
agaagalix*, east wind, west wind; and *chaxatax*, an offshore wind.[4]

---

4   Macleish, Sumner. *Seven Words for Wind: Essays and Field Notes from Alaska's
Pribilof Islands.* Epicenter Press, 1997.

Yesterday it occurred to me that *rain* is not a particularly useful word to describe liquid precipitation in Alaska. At various times, we must make use of every word in the thesaurus—shower, sprinkle, flurry, sheets, streams, drizzle, mist, torrent, cloudburst, and flood.

The word for yesterday was *downpour*. My neighbors' decks and porches are strewn with blossoms pummeled from their baskets, and along Monastery Drive, the tall columns of fireweed bow almost perpendicular to the ground. Already, the blooms on the fireweed have started to wither, and they will soon be entirely spent. Alaskans call it "topping off," and it means the end of summer is near, though it is still early in August.

On this Sunday morning, the Feast of the Transfiguration, the skies have cleared, the sun is shining, and the air has that sweet, faint chill that feels like fall. At Liturgy, Fr. Alexander, a young priest/professor from St. Vladimir's Orthodox Theological Seminary, chants the Gospel reading, and then surprises us by standing before the altar and holding the heavy book in his arms while he preaches his sermon. He looks like a young Moses, just down from the mountaintop.

Like Jesus, Fr. Alexander says, who was both transfigured and crucified "in the flesh," we must also put to death the passions in our own flesh. Like Jesus' earthly body that was transformed before the eyes of His apostles, we the Church, His body, must also be transformed before the eyes of man, so that the world will see Him in us.

Fr. Alexander has been with us this past week, a guest speaker at our annual Eagle River Institute, teaching us about the Orthodox history of Russia. He began with the Emperor Constantine's vision of the cross at the Malvian Bridge and went on to the conversion of Prince Vladimir and the Rus, the rise of Russian monasticism in the nineteenth century, and the horrific trials of the twentieth-century Church under communism.

On this feast day, the altar is rich with vested clergy, and the words of the hymns rise with the clouds of incense. As the acolytes lead the priests and deacons in the Great Entrance, I think of the words of the Kievan emissaries, ten good and wise men, who were sent one thousand years ago by Prince Vladimir to investigate the great religions and to recommend one of them for his people.

The emissaries did as they were told and reported to the Prince what they had seen at the great church of Hagia Sophia ("Holy Wisdom") in Constantinople: "We knew not whether we were in heaven or on earth. For on earth there is no such splendor or beauty, and we are at a loss how to describe it. We only know that God dwells there among humans, and their worship is fairer than the ceremonies of other nations. And we cannot forget that beauty. Every man who has partaken of sweetness will not afterwards accept bitterness, and so we can no longer remain apart from it."

Prince Vladimir was persuaded, Russia's pagan idols were destroyed, and a new era of church history began.

The Church, of course, is all about *transformation* and *mystery* (a more familiar word to Western Christians is *sacrament*). At every Divine Liturgy, wine and bread are transformed into the Body and Blood of Christ; at ordination, a man is transformed into deacon or priest; at baptism, a sinner is washed clean. And in marriage, a man and woman become one flesh.

It is not uncommon for the St. John's community to schedule weddings in late August, just after the Dormition Fast (weddings are prohibited during fasting seasons), when the waning warmth of summer often allows us to celebrate afterward on the church lawn. If you have ever been to an Orthodox wedding or seen one in a movie, you know that it differs, quite dramatically in fact, from other Christian marriage rites. Like all Orthodox ceremonies, it overflows with symbolism and instruction. Its two most interesting and meaningful features are the crowning of the bride and groom, followed by their ceremonial dance.

The crowns—sometimes made of gold and jewels, sometimes as plain as a wreath of flowers—represent the glory and honor with which God crowns the couple, and symbolize their new life together as king and queen of a new household, one that is centered in Christ and which they should rule wisely. The crowns also recall the "crowns of martyrdom," because, in marriage, God calls husband and wife to die to their own individual wills and live for each other.

The last act before the removal of the crowns and the priest's blessing is the dance, during which the choir sings three troparia, which are collectively called the "Dance of Isaiah." The first song recalls the Prophet Isaiah, who danced with joy when he foresaw the birth of Christ. The next remembers the Forty Martyrs of Sebaste, who fought the good fight of faith and received the martyr's crown. Finally, the third hymn proclaims glory to Christ, our God.

As the choir sings, the priest leads the couple around the table on which are placed the Gospel, the Word of God, and the Cross, the symbol of our redemption. They circle the table three times, and in this way, the Church leads the couple in their first steps as husband and wife, reminding them to center their life together on the Word and the Cross, and, by the candles they hold in their hands, to follow the light of Christ.

At St. John's, a wedding ceremony usually includes a short homily—some advice from the priest for the young couple standing in front of him, and for every other married person within the sound of his voice. Some years ago Fr. Marc said a few words, which I have never forgotten, to a bridal pair. They are short, sweet, and straight to the point. Here is what he said:

> We have all heard of "tying the knot" into the "bonds of matrimony." As Orthodox Christians, we believe that all the grace necessary for marriage is given in the sacrament of matrimony. There are, however, three "knots" which are absent from the sacrament and which all married couples would do well to remember. The first is that husbands and wives are "knot" given the ability to read each other's mind. It is necessary instead for each to speak his or her own mind, honestly and lovingly, and then to be quiet and listen. Second, growth in marriage is "knot" automatic, but, just as the stewards in the Gospel had to go and fill the pots with water in order to see the miracle of the wine, marriage requires effort. Third, the married couple alone is "knot" self-sufficient to accomplish all that Christian marriage promises them. This is why their first steps as a married couple are, literally, taken in procession around the Gospel; it is to remind them that they must always rely on God's presence and work in their life together.

I think that sums it up pretty well.

ALONG THE WALLS OF OUR CHURCH SOCIAL HALL ARE dozens of wedding pictures, beginning with one of Fr. Harold and Barbara at their wedding in 1955 and continuing on through the years, capturing a moment in time for the married couples of St. John's. The faces in the pictures are all smiling, happy, and full of hope. There is a picture of Bill and me, looking impossibly young, cutting our wedding cake in our hometown in East Texas. Myles and Maris sit cross-legged on the Big House lawn; she wears flowers in her long hair and he is almost unrecognizable behind a huge cloud of beard. Sally and Dick are beaming as they sit side by side in the office of the state magistrate in Palmer, Alaska. And Tim and Tanna, both looking slightly dazed, grin at the camera as if they can't quite believe they are finally married.

Marriage is a journey, and sometimes, even the route to its starting point is a twisting and complicated one. Few of the married folks at St. John's traveled farther, figuratively speaking, than Tim and Tanna, whose story is fascinating because it illustrates perfectly the element of chance (or, as Christians prefer to call it, the mysterious will of God) at work in our lives.

Tim has lived in Alaska since he was six, when his dad landed a job in Delta Junction, packed everybody into the family van, and headed north. The job fizzled (to the relief of Tim's mom, after she saw the rusticity and remoteness of Delta Junction), so Dad took the family to Anchorage and found a job right away. They moved into a nice, middle-class Anchorage neighborhood and worshipped at the Nazarene church.

Meanwhile, in Colorado, a young lady named Tanna grew up in a different sort of family. Her father was an intellectual, a lawyer and a judge. He had political aspirations, and, to further his career goals, the family attended the Presbyterian church. When Tanna was six, her parents divorced, and her dad left the Presbyterians to join the New Age movement.

Tanna chose to attend a "hippie boarding school" and spent summers and holidays alternately with her father and mother. During her teen years, a family tragedy led her to attend the Nazarene church, and she was accepted at Nazarene Bible College in California. Before starting classes, she took a summer job at a Colorado guest ranch, where she worked with Harley, the son of the ranch's owners, and his wife Diane.

Harley and Diane were excited. They had listened to teaching tapes by one of the seven men engaged in the "phantom search for the perfect church." They planned to move to Eagle River, Alaska—where Harold and Marc Dunaway were also involved in the search for the Church—and live there in the Big House. They shared the tapes with Tanna, who was so impressed by what she heard that she dropped her college plans and went with them.

Tim, meanwhile, followed his own, more orderly path. He graduated from high school in Anchorage, from college in California, and from law school in Oregon. For many years, he has practiced his profession at the office of the Alaska attorney general, researching, writing, and arguing criminal appeal briefs.

Tim always figured he would get married someday, but he laid down for himself two conditions that would have to be met: he would wait until he was financially secure, and he would not, under any circumstances, marry a woman with children. He liked his quiet, predictable life, and he often worked seven days a week. He spent Sunday mornings in his comfortable condo, relaxing and reading the newspaper. He called his peaceful home his "kingdom."

In Eagle River, Tanna lived for five years in the very different routine of the Big House—sharing space with others, learning to work out conflicts, participating in the community's journey toward Orthodoxy—while at the same time earning her LPN certificate and working at an extended care facility. She married, had three children, and was expecting the fourth when she made the hard decision to divorce from her husband.

Tanna and her children moved into a small duplex in the St. John's community. She describes herself as a "messy" person and recalls her household back then as somewhat less than orderly, but not quite out of control. She preferred spending time with her children to worrying about housework. Raising four children stretched her thin, but she never had to go it completely alone. Neighbors looked out for her, babysat her children, and helped clean her house.

Early on, Tanna resolved that she would not date while her children were young. She went back to college, earned her RN degree, and returned to work, but even as the children got older, she had deep, significant fears about remarrying, and doubted that there was a "right" man for her.

Tim, still living a calm, organized bachelor's life, continued to wait for his self-imposed conditions to be met before he would consider marriage. Though it often seemed that work was all he did, he found time here and there for a social life, and a friend introduced him to her co-worker, Laurie. Laurie, in turn, introduced him to her church, St. John's Orthodox in Eagle River, and to her friend, Phebe, a good friend of Tanna's. Tim admitted to Laurie and Phebe that he was open to the possibility of marriage, but that he would *never* marry a woman with children, *especially* teenaged children.

Tim was interested in St. John's and attended catechism classes, where Orthodoxy "started making sense" to him, and in due time he was chrismated. At the wedding of Eloise's grandson Joe, Tim sat next to her at the reception. As they chatted, he commented that he respected a man like Joe who was willing to marry a woman who already had children. In no uncertain terms, Eloise said she *thanks God* for such men. Years ago, her second husband Johnny adopted her four small children, and their lives, she told Tim, had been blessed by Johnny's presence. Tim was impressed by her fervent words, but he did not expect to emulate either Joe or Johnny.

It was at that wedding reception, celebrated on the church lawn under a blue sky and dazzling sun, that Phebe introduced Tim and Tanna to each other. Sparks didn't exactly fly. But it wasn't long before they began "seeing" each other; neither called it "dating." That changed when they decided to admit that a serious relationship was developing. Soon they were talking about marriage, but wondered: Would it be possible to merge their incredibly different households? Tim decided to talk it over with his dad.

"I'm considering marriage to a woman with four teenaged children," Tim said. They discussed the obstacles presented by this circumstance, and his dad concluded that while the situation would be a challenge, he was confident that Tim and Tanna could handle it.

"Thanks, Dad, I appreciate that," Tim replied. "By the way, she's also a registered Democrat."

Dad, a lifelong Republican, answered decisively. "Son, there are some differences that just *can't* be worked out." It was a lighthearted moment that helped Tim put things in perspective.

For her part, Tanna still wondered if she was capable of choosing the right man. But she was reassured by the support and positive encouragement of her church and community.

Tim and Tanna were married five years ago at St. John's. Blending the households has been every bit the challenge they expected. Tim has had to do a lot of adjusting and letting go of his "neatness issues." He had to learn to let the kids keep their rooms the way they wanted to, even though their way was not his way. A friend visited him and Tanna and the kids in their new house, looked around, and asked Tim if this was his new "kingdom." Tim laughed and said no, that he now lives in a "loosely held fiefdom."

As for the teenagers that Tim once vowed to avoid, things have worked out well. Since they had not grown up with a father they saw regularly, Tim feels lucky that he wasn't replacing someone else. The kids have expressed their gratitude that Tim came into their mom's life. Nina, now 23, said that in the days before Tim, her family seemed to be trying to balance on a two-legged stool. Tim, she says, became the third leg.

Tim and Tanna traveled over two very different roads to meet at the altar at St. John's. At first glance, it seems impossible that two such different people could ever become one. But it has worked. Tanna loves being bonded with a man who wants to be with her and who shares her values. Tim is glad that he didn't wait any longer to get married. His life now is a "whole new universe" and, had he been any older when he started the adventure, he might have lacked the patience that was required of him. They are different in lots of ways, but there is one thing on which they always agree: their marriage is a miracle.

Thomas à Kempis, a Catholic monk of the late Middle Ages, wrote *The Imitation of Christ*, one of the world's best known books on Christian devotion. He observed, "The resolutions of the just depend on the grace of God, rather than on their own wisdom; and in Him they always put their trust, no matter what they do. For man proposes but God disposes; nor is the way of man in his own hands."

In his own wisdom, Tim made a plan for his future, a future that would be orderly, predictable, and financially secure. Tanna, in her wisdom, told herself that she would likely never find the man who was both right for her *and* accepting of her children. They proposed but, as it turned out, God disposed.

Be exalted, O bridegroom, like Abraham; and be blessed like Isaac; and multiply like Jacob, walking in peace, and keeping the commandments of God in righteousness.

MYSTERY AND TRANSFORMATION

And you, O bride: Be exalted like Sarah; and exult like Rebecca; and multiply like Rachel; and rejoice in your husband, fulfilling the conditions of the law; for so is it well-pleasing to God.

—FROM THE ORTHODOX MARRIAGE SERVICE

GET UP AND MOVE

SEPTEMBER

EXALTATION OF THE CROSS

*O Lord, save Your people and bless Your inheritance, granting to the faith-
ful victory over their enemies, and by the power of Your cross preserving
Your habitation.*

—TROPARION OF THE FEAST

THE DUNAWAY FAMILY, IN TRAINING FOR CAMPUS CRUSADE
for Christ ministry, arrived at CCC headquarters in San Bernardino,
California, on a hot summer night in 1968. Barbara told me that as
they were settling into their hotel room, they watched television cov-
erage of the assassination of Robert Kennedy in Los Angeles. Earlier
that year, Martin Luther King had been murdered on a motel balcony
in Memphis. The Manson killing spree would horrify the country the
following summer.

But those were only a few pieces of the wild kaleidoscope of
unrest that was the late sixties. There were the Summer of Love, peace
demonstrations, civil rights demonstrations, Woodstock, Chappa-
quiddick, the generation gap, and the first moon landing. The sexual

revolution, the Jesus revolution, and the feminist revolution would soon be joined by the revolution for homosexual rights.

When Campus Crusade posted him to Alaska, Harold found himself in a prime mobilization area for U.S. troop deployment to Vietnam. Thousands of men and women passed through the state's military bases on their way to and from Southeast Asia. An early letter to their friends and family back home tells what those first weeks in Anchorage were like:

> There have already been several times we have asked ourselves, "Why are we here?" Each time a certain cloud seems to envelop us. But we knew there was a reason, and we trusted Him to show us why He has brought us here. We met a sergeant who agreed to give us a tour of the Post. There was row upon row of barracks and living quarters as far as the eye could see. Movement was at a standstill. It was only three in the afternoon but already it was dark, as old Sol had retired for the day. It is a cold and lonely place. Then we knew why we were in Alaska. Somehow, we had to get inside and share the warmth of a personal relationship with God through Christ.

Not long after he arrived, Harold toured the state's remote military bases, witnessing to the soldiers about Jesus Christ and salvation. As an evangelization tool, he used a film about another uprising, the peaceful one led by Christians in pursuit of the kingdom of God. The film was called *Revolution Now*, and, unknown to Harold, it had already caught the attention of the FBI. It was in Adak, far out on the Aleutian Islands, that Harold was fingered by the military police on suspicion of subversive activity and placed under house arrest. The Army commandeered the film for investigation. Fortunately, everything was sorted out (the film shared a title with another one that advocated certain countercultural political activity), and Harold was released after a few hours.

I'm telling this story to set the stage for another one, a story about a man, a child of the sixties, who was a "peacenik" and a searcher. He wasn't looking to overthrow anything, but rather to build something. He was looking for a community, and he undertook an amazingly determined search for it.

Harold P. (yes, a third Harold!) is a tall, lanky fellow who speaks softly and only when he believes he has something worth saying. He's a native of New England who lived for six years during his boyhood in Fairbanks, Alaska. He is retired from a career with the post office and enjoys flying small planes. He says that his life has been a journey in search of the truth, and he has logged many miles and crisscrossed the continent to find it.

I will begin Harold's story in upstate New York in the fall of 1967. The Vietnam War was escalating and his local draft board was calling. He saw Vietnam as a civil war in which the United States had no legitimate role, so he applied for conscientious objector status. He did not have a religious background, and when the draft board turned him down, he appealed. He was nineteen years old.

Harold decided to stay on the move while the appeal of his draft status was pending. In the spring of 1968, he landed in Berkeley, California, where he joined an activist peace group. He was broke, by his own choice, often hungry, and sometimes shoeless. But Berkeley, with its noise and movement and political ferment, fascinated him. He participated in a peace demonstration, was arrested, and then released to await trial. The peace group broke up, and although he believed in its ideals, he realized that shared political views would never be enough to hold a community together.

He heard about a fledgling community in Boulder, Colorado, so he went there, but found it was just a bunch of guys hanging out together. They told him about a Quaker farming group in British Columbia. That sounded good, so he went. He found a group of likeable people living in an idyllic setting, but he knew he couldn't live outside of the country until his two legal problems were resolved.

Harold remembered his boyhood years in Alaska, and he longed to go back there and live in the wilderness. In the fall of 1968, he stood trial on the Berkeley demonstration charges and was released, freeing him to head north to Alaska and await resolution of his draft appeal. First, however, he detoured to New Mexico to check out yet another community that sounded promising. It was in a spectacular setting in a ghost town, but the people there were just scraping by and seemed to lack a focus, so he left and went back to Boulder. He was still very philosophical, very optimistic about his search for truth about himself and about life.

In Boulder, he shelved his plans for Alaska in favor of another go at community. He recalls sitting with friends in a graveyard, where every-one committed themselves to stick together and try to get something going, in Canada maybe. To go with them, Harold needed money, so he stuck around and found work.

During the winter, the Boulder group dissolved, so Harold hitch-hiked back to British Columbia and spent the summer of 1969 with the Quakers. The appeal of his draft board's decision was still grind-ing through the system. His draft status—and his future—remained in limbo.

Once again, he returned to Boulder, where he got word that his final appeal for non-combat service had been denied. He decided to emigrate to Canada, or maybe Sweden, but something—he can't say exactly what it was—made him go to the army induction center in Denver and submit to the required physical exam. He was given forms to fill out, and in the margins he wrote paragraphs detailing his personal beliefs about war. He also snapped pictures of the place, which was not allowed, and was finally taken aside by the colonel in charge for a very long, very serious talk.

The colonel took Harold to the "moral waiver" office, which was run by a civilian who had taken classes in handwriting analysis. An examination of Harold's handwriting revealed that he was not violent and did not represent a threat to the nation. At the end of a long day, the United States Army granted Harold a "moral waiver," exempting him from immediate duty and returning his case to the local draft board for a change in status. After months of uncertainty, Harold was free to follow his dream to Alaska.

He spent the summer of 1970 in a remote cabin north of Denali National Park, and found he enjoyed living in simplicity and solitude. It gave him the opportunity to discover whether his thoughts and ideas were coming from within himself or from people around him. He was sure that the fundamental idea for the best way to live had to come from one's own heart, not from the advice or beliefs of others.

He recalls lying outside on a cold evening in early fall. He had watched many displays of the *aurora borealis*, but on this particular night, the light danced in ways he had never before seen. The center of the display was a great wheel of color, its spokes radiating from a central hub, that alternated between green and red as it slowly revolved in the night sky. Around the wheel were glowing, undulating ribbons of light, and as he watched, these too changed from milky green to reddish pink, and back to green again.

The sight entranced him and inspired in him a feeling of strength, a conviction that he could make it, that he would eventually find the answers he sought to his questions about how to live in this world. He also knew, as he watched that shimmering wheel above him, that God was working in his life, and he realized with certainty that it was in the wilderness of Alaska that he could learn the things God wanted to teach him.

Years later, Harold remembers the epiphany he experienced that night, and he connects it with what he has learned as an Orthodox Christian about God's revelation of Himself. Man and nature, Harold says, are not meant to be divided, at odds with one another. He enjoys reading of the many saints who stress the importance of man's connectedness with the rest of the created world, and who found in nature a sense of peace and wholeness. He points also to the Wise Men who, in the words of the Nativity troparion, "adored the stars," and who, by determinedly following a large and unusual one, "were taught to worship You, the Sun of righteousness."

Shortly after that night of the northern lights, Harold made plans to spend the winter in Anchorage. In spite of the many disappoint- ments in his search for community, he had not lost hope of finding it. He was beginning to understand that none of the groups he had investigated offered a good enough reason for people to stay together for the long haul. In Anchorage, he visited a few Protestant churches, which were full of nice people, but he saw some hypocrisy: People lived one way six days a week and another way on Sundays. He knew that there were Christians out there who were also serious seekers for truth, but his hope for finding the right community for himself was, at last, growing a bit dim.

Then he crossed paths with a guy who needed a roommate, who introduced him to a girl, who invited him to a Bible study at Harold and Barbara Dunaway's home on Fern Street in Anchorage. He went, and he got excited about what was going on there. The people he met seemed serious, and, more important, genuine.

Harold was tempted to stay in Anchorage, but his love for the solitude he found in the wilderness pulled him back to the Bush. He was still determined to discover who he really was, and to do it alone. Back in his cabin, his days were taken up with the hard work that it took to maintain even the simplest lifestyle.

One evening, after a long and tiring day spent hauling wood, he sat in his cabin and experienced another epiphany. Although his thoughts as he worked alone that day had seemed significant and far reaching, he realized that he could not easily put them into words. Words, he decided, can get in the way of clear thinking; it's hard to use them to express one's thoughts. But that discovery was followed by an even more important one. He also came to understand that it was a good God who created him to be the way he was, and it was that same good God who created everyone else to be the way they are. All of us, he realized, are basically alike in our desires and our dreams and our weaknesses. It was then that he knew the time had come when he was *really* ready to make a commitment to community. He decided to head back to Anchorage and find the Dunaways.

He found them, along with a few others, now living together in the Big House in Eagle River. At first, he was skeptical that he could stay there with them, and he decided to bolt, to head back to the Bush. But a broken-down car kept him in Eagle River. He moved into the Big House and joined in the study and discussion that was going on. He liked that part, but not the rest of it—the middle-class, suburban lifestyle, buying food at the grocery store, working to pay the bills. But he stayed.

He has been here since 1974. He and Barbara married and bought their home on nearby Darby Road, where they raised three children. Now that he's retired, they spend a lot of time at their rustic cabin on Katie Lake, cooking on a wood-burning stove and savoring the simplicity of the life they enjoy there.

Living what Harold calls a "suburban lifestyle" in Eagle River still goes against his grain, but he is willing to do it because he believes in the community and in the journey we are making together. He remembers the community's conversion to Orthodoxy as a series of proposed changes that were presented to the people, but were not adopted until everyone was ready. This, he says, happened because life here is about commitment to each other, not to the lone individual.

He sometimes misses the days before the building of the cathedral, when small groups met in "house churches." People were more tightly connected, and it was not easy to drop out of sight. The needs of the members were tended to more efficiently. Growth in numbers has made it necessary for folks to speak up and make their needs known, and not everyone is able to do that.

Harold knows that this community is not perfect. It's not the perfect place for him, but he is grateful that God has provided it. He doesn't stay because this is the most ideal place for him to live. He stays, he says, because, after almost forty years, "we're starting to have some history together in our journey toward God and His kingdom."

Depending on your point of view, Harold's singular quest for genuine community invites either admiration or scorn. After all, most of us raise our kids to follow a fairly set pattern—education, followed by employment, followed by putting down roots and becoming a productive citizen. But Harold was either intelligent enough or crazy enough—again depending on your point of view—to do it backward.

He knew, early on, that his first job as an adult was to discover how best to live. All the rest, he found out, would fall into place.

IT OCCURS TO ME THAT HAROLD P., WHO WAS NOT AFRAID to stand up and march in support of his beliefs, must have felt at home when he discovered that same action taking place in the Orthodox Church. I was never one to march for causes (except for the time I played a hippie in a church youth choir musical—I wore love beads and granny glasses, and walked around carrying a sign that said "Down with Everything!"). But I was born and raised in the Southern Baptist church, and I still love those foot-stomping old hymns like "Marching to Zion" and "Onward Christian Soldiers." At Vacation Bible School, our theme song was a rollicking anthem called "Assurance March," and to this day I can sing every word of every verse. Back then, we did a lot of singing about marching, but the Baptists I knew were not a physically demonstrative bunch, so we never really got up and moved.

Now, in the Orthodox Church, we get up and *march*, frequently. Well, actually, we *process*, which is more like walking on parade, because it is accompanied by singing and the carrying of banners and symbols. We process around the cathedral on certain feast days and to the cemetery for burials. Priests, deacons, and acolytes make two processions, the "Little Entrance" and the "Great Entrance," during every Liturgy.

Of all the ceremonial movement we do, the procession with lighted candles just before sunrise on Easter morning is probably the one dearest to our hearts. This one has it all: priests in rich white vestments carrying the heavy Gospel with its ornate gold cover; deacons bearing the crucifix, the icon of the Resurrection, and the smoking censer, its tinkling bells restored after the austerity of Lent; the faithful holding high our lighted candles and singing together, "Your Resurrection, O Christ our Savior, the angels in heaven sing: Enable us on earth to glorify You in purity of heart."

Our favorite moment happens when we complete our loop around the darkened cathedral and assemble in front of its wooden doors. Fr. Marc raises his heavy blessing cross and pounds three times on the door. "Open the gates!" he shouts, "that the King of Glory may come in!" Faithful K.C., who has played his role in this little drama for years, has remained inside the church so that he can reply, in a mysterious, muffled voice, "Who is this King of Glory?" And Fr. Marc's answer, loud and authoritative, always thrills me: "The Lord, strong and mighty! *He* is the King of Glory!"

The Cross, of course, is *the* central icon of the Church and is present in every procession we make. The Cross is celebrated pretty much constantly by the Orthodox, but its special day—the Feast of the Exaltation of the Cross—happens in September. If you change one letter in this feast's name, you get the word *exultation*. That is a good description of how we feel to see the Cross, lifted high and carried over Fr. Marc's head, as we sing about bowing down before it, and not only sing about it but actually do it, many times.

The September calendar is crowded with feast days. St. John the Evangelist (also called the "Divine" and the "Theologian"), patron of our Cathedral, is commemorated with another special procession around the church. This time, we all pause on each side of the cathedral while Fr. Marc says prayers of blessing for the building, then tosses big showers of specially blessed holy water on each wall before moving to the next.

Years ago, before processions and blessings with water were even imagined by the people here, one of those interesting, ironic coincidences (I once heard someone call them *God-incidences*) happened that is worth retelling. When the Dunaways lived on Fern Street in Anchorage in the late 1960s, they and their free-spirited group were turned off by the term "church." Had they been aware of Orthodoxy, they would no doubt have been doubly suspicious of an organization that called itself "*the Church*."

Oddly enough, there was a church right across the street and, what's more, it was St. Innocent's Orthodox Cathedral, usually called by Alaskans the "Russian" church. The Dunaway household watched the goings-on of the people across the way—their strange processions around the building, especially the one in the middle of the night at Easter with lighted candles and loud, clanging bells—and wondered just what kind of weird religion they practiced.

One night, overcome by curiosity, young Marc Dunaway and his friend Diane sneaked across the street and peeked through the windows of the church. They saw unfamiliar objects made of gold, strange and ornate paintings, and elaborately ornamented robes. Surely, they decided, these Orthodox must be a cult.

As the grownup Fr. Marc remembers that night, he laughs and admits that, to Fr. Nicholas Harris and his parishioners, the peculiar Protestants across the street from them must have seemed cultish as well. In one sense, Fr. Marc says, "we were both missionary families, but we were very different. We had come to this same Anchorage street from opposite directions on the globe. We read the same Bible and prayed to the same Christ, but we were worlds apart."

That furtive peek by two teenagers was the very first contact that the Dunaways would have with the ancient Orthodox Church. In the years to come, Fr. Nick Harris would become a dear friend of the St.

John's community, but back then his brand of ritualistic Christianity was the last thing the free spirits on Fern Street were interested in.

Little did they know then that one day they too would be a part of the Orthodox Church, and would be processing together around a cathedral of their own.

IF YOU SHOULD SOMEDAY TRAVEL TO EAGLE RIVER AND VEN-ture down Monastery Drive, look for the cemetery on your right, then beyond it for the blue roof and golden domes of a little Russian-style chapel on a hill. You will see a path beside the cemetery and, should you feel like taking a walk, you may follow the path through the woods and up a steep hill, where you can rest on a bench beside the chapel and listen to birds rustle among the trees.

I hope your visit brings you here during our brief, beautiful fall. By state fair time at the end of August, the fireweed has topped off and the leaves on the birches are turning to gold. If we are lucky, autumn will linger well into September and not be blown away early by the fierce winds that sometimes sweep down the Chugach Mountains and, overnight, tear the leaves from the trees.

It is mid-September, the feast day of St. Sergius of Radonezh, who committed his life to God while still a young boy and is greatly loved by the Russian people. This morning the students of St. John's School, along with their teachers, Fr. Marc, and anyone else who wants to go with them, will make a procession to the chapel for noon hour prayers.

On one day of each year, Fr. Marc says, he wears his purple velvet *skoufi*, the Russian priest's cap, in honor of St. Sergius. With Fr. Marc and Megan, who carries the icon of St. Sergius, in the lead, we process down the trail that passes the cemetery and winds through the thick trees. From the front of the column, Fr. Marc shouts, "Watch out for the bear poop!" All eyes look at the ground, and we step carefully around the two large piles. The trail takes us to the bottom of a steep hill, then through a grassy stretch of meadow before veering left and back into the trees.

The sun strains to break through in the overcast sky, and it is cold enough to make me wish I had grabbed my gloves. Beside the path, drops of water cling to the needles of a spruce tree like quivering diamonds. We smell the familiar fall odor of fat, shiny highbush cranberries and juicy rosehips that dangle like earrings from their vines. Nailed to a tree beside the path is an icon of St. Sergius. Fr. Marc stops to explain.

"This icon is here," he says, "to remind you to 'follow the saint.'"

To our right is a steep rock cliff, on top of which sits the chapel, and soon we are hiking uphill again. On a sharp turn leading to an even steeper stretch of trail, we come to a large carved cross with a small wooden bench beside it. The cross is the handiwork of Harold P., the man who refused to give up his search for community.

"This cross was carved from a spruce tree, the only tree that had to be cut down when we built the chapel," Fr. Marc tells us. "There's a cross here to remind us to keep on going, to encourage us that we are almost there."

From the bottom of the hill, we can see the chapel on the bluff above us. It is small and exquisite, its sides covered in cedar, its steeply pitched roof covered in blue painted cedar shakes. Two gold "onion" domes, topped by metal crosses, rise above the trees.

Fr. Marc stops the procession on the porch and points out the angel above the door. It is a wooden carving of one of the mysterious seraphim, encircled by its six wings, and I think of the words of my favorite hymn, the one we sing before the Great Entrance at Liturgy on Holy Saturday, and the last verse that always gives me goosebumps: "At His feet the six-winged seraph, cherubim with sleepless eye, veil their faces to the presence, as with ceaseless voice they cry: Alleluia, Allelulia, Alleluia! Alleluia Lord Most High!"

One by one, the children stop to kiss the icon of St. Sergius before going in and taking their places in the chapel's tiny nave that smells of cedar and incense. Over our heads is the eight-armed chandelier with its many candles, and higher up the walls, two stained glass windows face each other. Each depicts a cross before a gray sun, to commemorate the day of Christ's crucifixion "when the sky became dark." On the iconostasis in front of us is a large icon of St. Sergius, holding in his hand a small version of our chapel that bears his name. Fr. Marc slips on his gold-colored stole and faces the icons, and we say the prayers for St. Sergius.

When the prayers are done, he tells us a story about the saint. One day, while praying in a small church very much like this one, the monk Sergius felt afraid, as if he was under a spiritual attack by enemies he could not see. And here is how he fought his fear: He spoke aloud the words of the Paschal hymn, "Let God arise! Let His enemies be scattered!" And at once, Fr. Marc says, Sergius felt calm and peaceful again. "Now look up at the wall," Fr. Marc says, and we raise our eyes to the words painted in a circle around us. They are the very words of the hymn that Sergius used to scatter the enemies of God that frightened him.

It is time for the children to go back to school, and Fr. Marc tells them to notice, on their way out, the marks on the corner of the north wall. A silly bear, he said, got a whiff of the newly stained wood and must have thought it would be good to eat. The marks of his teeth are still there, along with scratches left by his claws.

Their pilgrimage is over, and the children head down the hill while I remain behind for a few minutes, sitting on the little bench and watching the wispy line of clouds that drifts halfway down the mountains. A light breeze sends an occasional golden leaf floating to the ground, which is dotted with big red mushrooms.

Gradually, the noisy chatter and laughter of the children recedes in the distance, and the only sound is the low hum of traffic from the invisible highway beyond the trees.

With a last look at the words carved above the cross on the chapel door—*King of Glory*—I follow the children home.

MARY AND JUDY, WHO CAME TO LIVE IN THE COMMUNITY AT St. John's around the same time and who are about the same age, share a special love for the St. Sergius Chapel.

Seventeen years ago, Mary was living in Mississippi and struggling through some hard times. She was single, an Orthodox Christian, and her brother-in-law, a priest, had heard good things about the St. John's community and the Big House. He suggested to her that she make a fresh start in a brand new place. She trusted his advice, so with "fear and trepidation," but with hope also, she left everything behind her and boarded a plane for Alaska.

It was hard, at first. Five thousand miles from everything and everyone she had ever known, she gave up a spacious apartment she shared with her brother and moved into a small suite with five strangers.

Judy, meanwhile, was living and working in Eagle River and

enjoying her "party lifestyle." That is, she used to enjoy it, but was starting to realize that it left her unsatisfied, wanting something more. She was a hairdresser, and one of her clients, Jennifer, invited her to a service at St. John's and introduced her to Fr. Paul. Judy casually told him that she would think it over and get back to him if she was interested in his church.

But Fr. Paul, a persuasive priest, did not wait to hear from her. Like a river kayaker who hits unexpected rapids, Judy found her world rocking back and forth and sometimes even turning upside down. She moved in with two other young women on Monastery Drive, and a short time later was baptized and chrismated. Eventually, she moved into the Big House, and it was there, she says, that she finally found out who she really was.

Judy thought of herself back then as "a together sort of person." A few months of life in the Big House changed that. "Being the oldest in the House does not grant automatic immunity from shoveling snow or butchering a moose at 2:00 A.M.," she wrote in a newsletter at the time. "And if you have any weakness in your character (and you do, believe me), it will surface and rise before you and the other people you live with." Sharing a bathroom with five other girls and a bedroom with one of them, a fourteen-year-old, she lost her "togetherness." Like Mary, one of her roommates, Judy found life in the House pretty hard, at first.

Mary and Judy shared a love for art and for the creative life, and both enjoyed making things with their hands. They and the other House residents cleaned their home together, cleaned the church together, and worshipped together. Judy says that those activities, along with their participation in community weddings, births, and deaths, taught them to live a Christian life in actions as well as words.

Construction of the chapel started during their first summer at the Big House. It was designed by a Russian artist and his wife who, along with their children, left Moscow in the early 1990s and lived and worked for a time in the St. John's community. Yuri Sidorenko—a classically trained painter, iconographer, and architect—and his wife, Vera, a folk artist, no longer live here, but they left behind them a beautiful legacy.

(In our living room, hanging over Grandma Cook's old buffet, is one of our treasures—a painting by Yuri, a still life of jewel-colored flowers, fruit, and wine, painted in the mesmerizingly realistic "old Russian masters" style. The grapes and peaches glisten, as if just washed, and the roses glow in a soft light.)

Like the cathedral, the chapel was built by the community, and it was no small feat. On a high, wooded bluff several hundred yards off Monastery Drive, the chapel sits on a large stone outcropping; since a foundation could not be dug, the building had to be attached to rock. The chapel's construction workers had no road access to the site. They made do with a rough, narrow trail, part of it on a steep, slippery hill. Judy recalls walking with pack crews who dragged construction materials by hand to the site.

(My son Justin, who was still in high school at the time, worked with the crew that hoisted the domes into place. He remembers standing on the chapel's roof and gazing across the valley that lies between the chapel and the cathedral. The trees were at their peak of fall glory, and the small blue-and-gold building seemed to float in a sea of vivid yellow foliage. It is a sight he will never forget.)

Mary says it was Fr. Harold's idea that Judy, an accomplished woodcarver, should create a large angel to be placed above the chapel door. Judy, willing and obedient, sketched a plan, found a suitable block of wood, and went to work. All through the summer, the angel was a work in progress. Visitors often dropped in to the girls' apartment to watch as the angel took shape.

As each piece of the chapel was finished—doors, windows, icons, domes, chandelier, and, eventually, Judy's angel—it was brought to the cathedral for all to see and admire. On September 17, 1993, the icons of the chapel's iconostasis, painted by Yuri, were on display in the cathedral when the community at St. John's received an unusual guest.

On a splendid green and gold fall afternoon, three white stretch limos turned onto Monastery and drove slowly into the parking lot of the cathedral. Inside one of the limos was Aleksy II, Patriarch of Moscow, in Alaska for the first stop on a three-week American tour. In his entourage were a half-dozen security men from the U.S. State Department, a Russian television crew, and fourteen other Orthodox clergy.

Earlier that afternoon, the patriarch had visited St. Nicholas Church in the tiny village of Eklutna, population 35, just up the road from St. John's. St. Nicholas was founded in the 1870s as a permanent place of worship for the nomadic Athabascan Indians. Patriarch Aleksy was headed to the Russian Cathedral in Anchorage, and Fr. Nick, priest at St. Innocent's, arranged for the patriarch to stop off on the way for a short visit with us.

Everyone who could make it was on hand to greet him. We stood in the cathedral singing the hymn to the Theotokos as he came in, an imposing, bearded man wearing a black cassock and a white-and-gold *klobuk*, or monastic headdress. He walked slowly to the front of the nave, took off his *klobuk*, and bent to kiss the altar. Through a translator, we listened as he blessed us, and then said prayers of blessing for the icons that would soon be installed in St. Sergius Chapel. He called the chapel "a spiritual bridge between our two countries."

Even though Russian missionaries came to Alaska over two hundred years ago, Aleksy II was the first head of the Russian Orthodox Church ever to visit our state during his reign. I believe he was probably as surprised to see us, a parish of American Orthodox converts, as we were to see him. The story of the patriarch's visits that day made the front page of the *Anchorage Daily News*, complete with a picture of the St. John's faithful, waving goodbye as his limo headed out on Monastery.

Eventually, the day came—September 25, 1994, the feast day of St. Sergius—when the little jewel of a chapel was finished and finally blessed by His Grace, Bishop Basil Essey. St. John's folks visit the chapel often, and visitors and tourists are always welcome to hike the steep, twisting trail and see it for themselves. Every Thanksgiving morning, Fr. Marc leads a group of parishioners across the icy path to pray the Akathist of Thanksgiving together in the candlelit chapel.

Judy no longer lives in the St. John's community. She is a nun at the Monastery of the Transfiguration in Ellwood City, Pennsylvania, and she is now called Mother Mary. Her time at the Big House, she says, helped form her for the life she lives today. At the House, she learned to ask forgiveness of others and to work through conflict. It was there that she realized, painfully, that she was "out of youth's inner circle," and it was time to stop messing around and do something with her life.

Mary is still here, struggling as we all do from time to time, but staying on. She is a familiar sight in the community, dressed in her long coat and one of the hats she loves to wear. She walks frequently and, even in winter, enjoys visiting the chapel. The chapel, she says, graces and blesses the woods that surround it. Judy's angel, she believes, protects it and guards it. Mary's first months in the St. John's community were not easy ones, but she is still here, and many good things have happened in her life since then. But she will always remember that first summer, the summer of the angel.

> *Let there always be quiet, dark churches in which man can take refuge, places where he can kneel in silence, houses of God filled with his silent presence.*
>
> —THOMAS MERTON

EVERYONE'S HOME

OCTOBER

HOLY FATHERS OF THE SEVENTH ECUMENICAL COUNCIL

The Son who shone forth from the Father was ineffably born, twofold in nature, of a woman. Having beheld Him, we do not deny the image of His form, but depict it piously and revere it faithfully. Thus, keeping the True Faith, the Church venerates the icon of Christ's Incarnation.

—KONTAKION OF THE FEAST

IF YOU'RE LIKE ME, YOUR HOUSE WILL NEVER BE READY FOR company. It will always be too small, too messy, too ugly, too uncomfortable, too crowded, too something. I love the *idea* of drop-in guests, but I confess that I squirm when it actually happens. My mind churns with silent questions: What is the condition of the bathroom? Do I have anything in the refrigerator to offer besides a half-used bottle of wine that was plugged last week with a wad of plastic wrap? And why haven't I vacuumed those huge dog hair tumbleweeds from the corner?

Hospitality-challenged people like myself love to pretend that the vision of the perfect hostess welcoming guests to her perfect house is just that, a vision, and that this mythical goddess exists only in the pages of a magazine. Deep down, we know this is untrue. It is simply a fact that there are women (and men) who know how to make guests, unexpected or not, feel welcomed and cared for. They have enough poise not to babble apologies about the dirty dog, the dubious toilet, or the forlorn fridge. They have a gift of hospitality.

Barbara Dunaway knows how to take care of guests. She learned from her Kentucky grandmother, a fervent Christian who often entertained Methodist pastors in her farmhouse. Barbara loved her grandparents' home; she was inspired by it, as she was by Edith Schaeffer's L'Abri, to create her own "place with purpose," an open home where hospitality is provided at the drop of a hat.

Jenny, one of the first nine young adults to live at the Big House, recalls the evenings she spent in Barbara's Fern Street home in Anchorage:

> The house was usually full, so I wiggled my way into a corner of the living room or found a place on the stairway. It was more than just the message, the occasional rabbit stew, and the camaraderie that kept me coming back. I had never experienced the sort of welcome that Harold and Barbara shared with everyone. In their home, I saw that a table set for five could become a table serving twenty-five, an art of hospitality that I have yet to learn.

Mike, a young Elmendorf AFB airman in 1971, also spent time at Barbara's Anchorage home, where he experienced not only her generosity at dinnertime, but also her willingness to give advice when it was needed. She once asked him what he wanted in life. A wife, he told her. "Well, Mike," she replied, "maybe someday God will make you the type of man that a woman will want to marry."

"That," he says, "took a while to digest."

Barbara was seriously challenged by a constant frustration, the lack of a water source for the Big House, caused by the great Alaska earthquake of 1964 that dried up the house's well. There was some relief when a neighbor, who was blessed with a bottomless well, agreed to allow them to run a plastic pipe one thousand feet from his well to the tanker car buried in the Big House front yard. This chore had to be done twice a week, in snow, rain, and below zero temperatures. Water was strictly rationed.

But Barbara and her household were not the first ones in the house to be nagged by the water problem. Five years before they bought the place, it had been owned by the Catholic Church and was home to six nuns, whose ascetic struggle also included coping with the bothersome water shortage. But, although the people in the Big House never met them, the significance of the nuns in the St. John's story goes way beyond the shared frustration over water.

A visitor to the guest room of the Big House will see on the wall a large black-and-white photograph of a middle-aged, balding man who wears the black-and-white robe of a monastic order. He looks straight into the camera and smiles so broadly that you just know he is about to laugh at something. His picture hangs there to commemorate his visit, forty years ago, to the nuns who lived in the big house at the end of Monastery Drive, where he recorded what he thought, what he saw, and what he said. His name was Thomas Merton.

Remember those dominoes I talked about that are carefully arranged, and when the first one is tipped, the others fall, revealing an intricate pattern? In the story of the St. John's church and community, the visit of Thomas Merton to the nuns is one of those dominoes. Or, as Maye says, it is like "connecting the dots." Sometimes, the search for history is like that. When we discover the stories of those who came before us, we discover a greater appreciation for the place where we are.

Thomas Merton was a Trappist monk of the Roman Catholic Church, and his name was familiar, and controversial, in the 1960s. He was a popular author of books on the contemplative life; his autobiography, *The Seven Storey Mountain*, became a bestseller in 1948 and is still in print. Although he lived for years within the confines of the Abbey of Our Lady of Gethsemani in Kentucky, he was both praised and criticized for his passionate anti-war activism and for his interest in Asian religions. I talked with an Eagle River man, a life-long Catholic, who put his objection to Fr. Merton's activism this way: "Thomas Merton took a vow of silence and didn't keep it."

In 1968, two changes in the rules of his order profoundly affected Fr. Merton's life. One made it possible for the monks of Gethsemani to maintain their ties to the Kentucky monastery while living at a distance from it. The other made it possible for Fr. Merton to fulfill his long-held desire to travel to Asia. In mid-September of that year, about the same time the Dunaway family of Kentucky arrived in California for Campus Crusade training, Fr. Merton left Kentucky, bound eventually for Thailand, where he planned to study with Eastern religious leaders. But before he went there, he would spend two weeks in another faraway place that fascinated him and where he considered establishing a secluded hermitage for himself. He would go to Alaska.

Meanwhile, another man had also been busy during the 1960s. Fr. Joseph Ryan, first Catholic Archbishop of Anchorage, had put out a call for nuns and priests to come north and join his young archdiocese. The bishop was especially interested in attracting monastics, and among the nuns who accepted his invitation were six contemplative Sister Adorers of the Precious Blood, who came north in 1967 from their mother house in Portland, Oregon. Their home in Alaska was the big house in Eagle River, near the end of the road that would eventually be named for them.

The sisters, veiled in their white habits with the red scapular, were excited to be in Alaska on a frontier mission field. The group included a musician, a painter, and a vestment maker. They called their community the "Northern Star," and, as contemplatives, their main occupations were supposed to be prayer and meditation. But it seems that from the start of their residence in Eagle River, they were expected to manage a full schedule of meetings and retreats at their convent house. In addition to their regular cycle of prayers and services, they also cooked, cleaned, and did laundry for their many guests. It was impossible for them to remain cloistered.

Their guests often included nuns of other orders, women who were educated and engaged in "important" work, such as teaching and nursing and administering Catholic charities. The young contemplative sisters of the Precious Blood knew about the changes happening as a result of Vatican II. They met nuns who no longer wore a traditional habit, who opted to keep the name they received at birth rather than accept a new one. They heard about nuns who visited other churches and were not rebuked for it. Some began to feel a sense of restlessness.

The "mother" of the convent was Sister Rita Mary, who was older and more seasoned than the other five. Before writing this story, I spent a good deal of time looking for her and was excited when I finally learned that she lived in Brooklyn, New York. But my excitement turned to sorrow when I telephoned her convent and learned that she had passed away only the day before.

The sisters there were kind enough to send me copies of Sister Rita Mary's letters, in which she mentioned Archbishop Ryan's concern for the welfare of his priests and sisters, fearing that some might suffer "cabin fever" in the cold and isolation. The bishop invited Thomas Merton to come and give them teaching and encouragement, and to help him find a suitable location in Alaska for a new monastery or hermitage in which to live.

While in Alaska, Fr. Merton kept a journal that is preserved, along with letters he wrote and transcripts of the teaching he did here, in a little book called *Thomas Merton in Alaska*.[5] The quotes that follow are taken from that book.

Fr. Merton spent his first four days in Alaska at the Precious Blood convent in Eagle River. He wrote in his journal, "The convent chapel looks out through big windows at birch, a purple and green mountainside. Quiet. Sense of belonging here. The spirit of the community is good." He loved to gaze at the snowy peaks of Mt. McKinley and, closer by, to explore the nearby mountains and trails. I imagine Fr. Merton sitting near the fireplace in the house's big living room, and the rapt attention of the sisters as they listen to him, and I am amazed to read his prophetic words. It is as if he also intended them to be heard by the different community that would be here years later.

He told the nuns: "[P]eople come here to find a group of people who love one another. They don't come here merely to see you as individuals; they come to see you as a community of love. If they are going

---

5   *Thomas Merton in Alaska: The Alaskan Conferences, Journals, and Letters,* New Directions, 1988.

to find grace and help, it isn't so much from each one of you as an individual, but from the grace that is present in a community of love."

The fact that the sisters *were* a community of love, in spite of whatever doubts and hardships they may have been enduring, is borne out by their neighbors. There are folks in Eagle River today who recall the warmth and friendliness of the sisters' kitchen and their gratitude for neighbors' gifts of fresh-caught salmon and home-grown vegetables. They remember the nuns' devotion as they prayed in their tiny, candle-lit chapel. Their house, like the Big House it has now become, was a welcoming place to the many friends, guests, and retreat visitors it received.

After leading six workshops in Eagle River, Fr. Merton moved to the archbishop's residence in Anchorage, where he stayed between short trips around Alaska. He visited Cordova, Yakutat, Juneau, and Dillingham, meeting the local clergy, sometimes celebrating Mass, and scouting locations for a hermitage. He described the Alaskans he met as "good, simple people . . . not yet caught up in the mess of problems which are found in the States." (If only that had ever been true!)

Of Cordova, a picturesque little fishing village east of Anchorage on Prince William Sound, he wrote, "Eyak Lake seemed perfect" and "in many ways the best place I have seen so far." In Yakutat, he met a man who promised to donate land for a monastery if Fr. Merton himself would run it. They "shook hands on the deal," and Fr. Merton told the man he would return in a couple of months.

Fr. Merton spoke to all the Anchorage area nuns at a Day of Recollection. Perhaps anticipating his journey to Asia, he told the sisters: "[O]ur life demands breakthroughs . . . once in awhile we must break through and go beyond where we are." Again, for those of us at

St. John's who have made significant changes in our lives on the way to our conversion to Orthodoxy, his words are hauntingly prophetic.

On October 1, the ground was covered with a light autumn snowfall when Thomas Merton left Alaska for a brief stay in California before continuing on to Asia. In letters written from Anchorage to his abbot, he described what he had seen here and added, "I think Alaska would be the best place in the U.S. for a hermitage," and "I hope I can return here when I am through in Asia." But what happened just two months later made it impossible ever to know for sure what he would have decided.

On December 10, 1968, Thomas Merton died in his Bangkok hotel room, a victim of accidental electrocution. The Alaska sisters, stunned by the news, were comforted by the memory of his parting promise to pray for them.

Among the many fascinating comments Fr. Merton made during his visit to the Precious Blood sisters was another surprisingly prophetic one. He told them of his interest in the theology of the Eastern Orthodox Church and his belief that it is "something that we might profitably explore in the present day."

Even more touching for us here at St. John's is a portion of another letter he wrote to his abbot: "[T]here is an old Russian Orthodox monk who has lived for years as a hermit off Kodiak Island and in fact before him there was a Staretz there who is venerated as a saint. . . . I was not able to get to Kodiak and this old monk is now sick . . . but I hope to meet him someday before he dies."

The *staretz* (a spiritual guide) of whom Fr. Merton spoke was the Monk Herman, the eighteenth-century Russian Orthodox missionary who brought Christianity to the Native people of Alaska and whose love and care for them inspired their devotion to him. Herman was, in fact, canonized in 1970 as the first Orthodox saint of North America and today is revered worldwide.

The "old Russian Orthodox monk" whom Fr. Merton hoped to meet was Fr. Gerasim, the "guardian" of St. Herman's memory. Fr. Gerasim first came to Alaska as a young monk in 1916. In 1935, he fulfilled the desire of his heart and moved to Spruce Island, where he kept alive the recollection and knowledge of Fr. Herman. Fr. Gerasim died there in October, 1969, less than a year after the death of Thomas Merton, and too soon to see the celebration of Fr. Herman's sainthood.

As I read Fr. Merton's journals and letters to his abbot, I am pierced with sadness and regret that he, apparently, did not meet any Orthodox person or visit any Orthodox church during his weeks in Alaska. How might history have been changed, I wonder, if he *had* made that visit to Spruce Island, if he *had* found in the Christian Church of the East the fullness of faith for which he searched.

But somehow, I know, a connection *has* been made. Though neither Fr. Merton nor those six busy nuns were aware of it, the seeds of community they planted in the big house on Monastery Drive would bear fruit decades later in our community of Orthodox Christians. Though we are not monastics, we who live here now deal with many of the same challenges faced by those who were here before us.

In their newsletter, the Precious Blood sisters wrote, "We have come to love this house and this locality, but are ready to move if we must." The lack of water forced them to move in 1970 to a new retreat center in Anchorage which they were asked to manage. They and their bishop soon realized that this work was not compatible with their contemplative calling, and a year later the group returned to their Portland mother house.

Though their stay here was brief, and though we are separated by time, death, and religious differences, the memory of Thomas Merton and the nuns remains poignant, as do the words of Fr. Merton, jotted quickly in his notebook just before his plane landed in Anchorage: "I am here in answer to someone's prayer."

We who have journeyed from the familiar, comfortable land of the church of our childhood and youth to the new and different land of Orthodoxy are easily able to identify with him in those times that "demand breakthroughs." Like Fr. Merton, we have, by God's grace, broken through and emerged into a place beyond, a place we love, a place to call home.

UNLIKE MY FAMILY'S OLD BAPTIST CHURCH, THE ONE THAT embarked on a campaign to "grow the membership," the St. John's church and community never drew up a master plan to attract people to come here. Like Harold P., most of us were drawn to this place by word of mouth—my family, you recall, lived in Anchorage for fourteen years without the slightest awareness of the place until we heard about it from a friend, who heard about it from a college classmate who lived on Monastery Drive.

Other stories are much more fascinating than ours. Joyce and her husband, Deacon Fred, lived in Eagle River in the early days of their marriage. She hungered for a church home but wasn't sure where to go. One Sunday morning, she got in her car and set out to find a church. She saw another driver, a woman who appeared to be dressed for and headed to some kind of service, so Joyce decided to follow.

All the way to Monastery Drive and then to the Big House at the end of the road, Joyce followed the woman's car. Later, she learned that it was Robin she followed, and the church she found was Grace

Community Church. Joyce and Deacon Fred and their children have been here ever since.

Deacon Dan and Theresa's friend, Brad, was a searcher who read *Becoming Orthodox* by Fr. Peter Gillquist during a cross-country flight. The book mentions St. John's in Alaska, and Brad remembered his old friend Dan who was stationed here. As soon as his plane landed in Boston, Brad phoned Dan and told him excitedly about a "convert" Orthodox church in Eagle River and urged him to go and check it out.

Dan and Theresa worshipped at an Assembly of God church back then and were not exactly church shopping. But they were open to possibilities and agreed to do as Brad advised. One frosty November evening they headed up Monastery to their first Vespers service, and they too have been here ever since.

Anna and Keith were newlyweds and stained glass craftsmen who worshipped at the Church of Christ, the church of Keith's ancestors. They sensed something missing in that place of worship, but did not know what the "something" was or how to find it. In their apartment one day, they prayed together and asked God to lead them to a church of His choosing.

As they got up off their knees, there was a knock at the door. It was their neighbor from across the hall, Robin (who, as I told you, is a woman who touches others' lives by sharing her own so generously), who wondered if they would be interested in creating stained glass windows for her church. Anna and Keith looked at each other, and both realized that something extraordinary had just happened.

A week later, Robin knocked again and invited Anna and Keith to the Big House for a teaching on the "Timeline of Church History." Anna went to the teaching, listened to the information that was presented, and knew immediately that she would go home and tell Keith that their prayer had been answered. Twenty-five years later, they are still here.

My good friend Steve, an energetic and successful salesman who came to Alaska years ago to indulge his fondness for rock climbing, was attending a Lutheran church in Anchorage when he took a job at the same car dealership that employed Joe, a long-time St. John's member. Steve and Joe became friends and, eventually, Joe invited Steve to check out a service. Steve was reluctant, and besides, his wife was a cradle Lutheran and content to stay there.

Joe didn't let the matter drop, however, and on a weekend when his wife was out of town, Steve decided to see what was happening at St. John's. From that first visit, he was hooked, but knew that his wife would need convincing. His birthday was coming up, and when she asked what he would like for a gift, he asked her to go to the Orthodox church in Eagle River with him. She did, they stayed, and eventually they moved into a log house perched on a mountainside a short distance from the cathedral.

Steve's faith and endurance were tested when his marriage ended in divorce, but his story contains some new chapters. Seven years ago, he married Ruth, a sweet and soft-spoken widow, and in their home on Monastery Drive, they have worked to blend their two young families. Steve has never wavered in his conviction that in finding the Orthodox Church and the community of St. John's, he found the place and purpose of his life.

Back in the 1970s, those seven men who were engaged in the "phantom search for the perfect church" were also issuing a "call to community." In a pamphlet titled *Coming in from the Cold*, Fr. Richard

Ballew wrote, "It was God who created the idea of community. God created human beings to live in community. We want to bring people back to community based on the Lordship of Jesus Christ."

Another of the original seven (who later dissociated from the group) was even more blunt in *A Call to Community*: "One of the great heresies of the twentieth century Church is its loss of community. Much of what we call 'church' has become a museum for loners; people have been programmed to avoid in-depth love for each other at least six days a week."

Forty years ago, a popular complaint among confused moderns was (and still is, I suppose) something called an "identity crisis," which meant that the afflicted person was unsure about who he was and where he fit into society. The leaders of the movement from Protestant evangelicalism to Orthodoxy believed they knew the reason for all this confusion. "It is impossible," Fr. Richard wrote, "to know fully who you are and how to relate to yourself unless you are in a community." Americans were losing their identity, he said, for two reasons: our growing tendency to move around a lot; and a culture of technology and consumerism that took our attention away from family and neighbors and focused it on entertainment.

And he wasn't the only one noticing these changes. Way back in 1972, just about the time the Dunaways and their friends were making an intentional move to Eagle River, a sociologist named Vance Packard was talking about some interesting new trends— shopping-mall and drive-in churches—that he connected to a concept taking hold in the minds of many Protestant leaders. Mr. Packard quoted from an editorial in *Christian Century*: "The churches cannot minister effectively to a mobile population if they cling nostalgically to traditional forms of architecture." The editor called for "a mobile church for a mobile people."[6]

When those early St. John's parishioners first began to form an intentional community, they were not Orthodox or even a *church* at all. But the faith they embraced and the church they built was about as far as you can get from the notion of "modern" and "mobile." Together, we are learning that life is not only about people and possessions. It is about *place.*

> [C]ommunity is first and foremost a gift of the Holy Spirit, not built upon mutual compatibility, shared affection or common interests, but upon having received the same divine breath, having been given a heart set aflame by the same divine fire and having been embraced by the same divine love.
>
> —HENRI NOUWEN
> (*BEHOLD THE BEAUTY OF THE LORD*)

---

6   Packard, Vance, *A Nation of Strangers*, David McKay Company, Inc., 1972.

A PLACE TO REST

NOVEMBER

FEAST OF THE PRESENTATION OF THE THEOTOKOS

Today is the prelude of God's good will and the prophecy of the salvation of men; in the Temple of God the Virgin plainly appears, and early proclaims Christ to all. To her let us cry out with loud voice: Rejoice, O fulfillment of the Creator's dispensation.

—TROPARION OF THE FEAST

ENCASED IN HARDENED RIPPLES OF ICE, MONASTERY DRIVE looks like the gray, corrugated tin that covers ramshackle houses in East Texas, my childhood home. The leaves have long since blown away, and our houses lie in the shadow of the mountains until early afternoon, when the pale sun finally clears their crest. But the sun will not remain in the sky for long—the days are short, counting down now until their lowest ebb.

It is Thanksgiving morning and the anniversary of the death of Fr. Lazarus Moore, whose earthly journey took him literally around the world before he chose to spend his final years with the community at

St. John's. In the dim, early morning light, around thirty well-bundled parishioners stand with Fr. Marc on the snowy ground of the cemetery, facing Fr. Lazarus's cross-shaped stone monument. We are here to say prayers and to sing "Memory Eternal." (Every time we sing that haunting, melancholy song, I feel as if I am on the windswept Russian steppe, watching and listening as a group of nineteenth-century villagers bears a coffin to the graveyard.)

In a snapshot taken of our family after our chrismation, we are seated close together, surrounding an elderly, frail-looking gentleman. The old man's hair falls nearly to his shoulders, and he wears a long black cassock. Through his old-fashioned glasses, he looks at the camera calmly, smiling a little in a bemused sort of way.

He is Archimandrite (archpriest-monk) Lazarus of blessed memory, who was born Edgar Harman Moore in Swindon, England, on October 18, 1902. After graduating from the Royal Agricultural College, he struck out for western Canada, and while working as a farm laborer in Alberta, received, in his own words, a "call from God." He returned to England to study at St. Augustine's Theological College and discovered his gift for linguistics, a skill that would serve him well throughout his long career. He was ordained a deacon in 1930 in the Church of England, and was made a priest one year later. Soon after, he joined a brotherhood in India, a place which would later take on even greater significance in his life.

During a visit to Jerusalem in 1934, Edgar came in contact with the Russian Orthodox Church Outside of Russia (ROCOR), and was eventually chrismated. Two years later, while in Serbia, he was tonsured an Orthodox monk and then raised to the priesthood. Back in Jerusalem, Fr. Lazarus quickly learned Russian and Church Slavonic and began the translation work for which he is justly remembered.

He remained in Jerusalem until 1948, when the new state of Israel turned over the ROCOR mission property in Jerusalem to the Soviet Union.

Fr. Lazarus returned to India in 1952 and remained there for the next twenty years, engaged in missionary work, translating, and writing. His translated works include *The Ladder of Divine Ascent*, by St. John Climacus; *The Psalter; The Arena,* by St. Ignatius Brianchaninov; and *The Russian Prayer Book,* often called *The Old Jordanville Prayer Book.* It was in India at that time that he met Mother Gabriella, with whom he consulted on his translation work. He authored a well-known biography, *St. Seraphim of Sarov—A Spiritual Biography,* now back in print.[7]

In 1983, Fr. Peter Gillquist invited Fr. Lazarus to California to assist with the integration of the former Evangelical Orthodox Church into canonical Orthodoxy. During a summer 1986 visit to St. John's in Alaska, Fr. Lazarus met two people with whom he would spend the last three years of his earthly life. Diane, an intense, energetic, and hospitable woman, immediately sensed a connection with Fr. Lazarus and began corresponding with him. When he needed to find a new place to live, she and her husband Harley talked it over and invited him to move to Eagle River and live with them.

Fr. Lazarus gave them a trial run, and they passed the test. Diane recalls that one of Fr. Lazarus's nephews protested his uncle's move to the arctic climate of Alaska. "God doesn't send us to heavens," Fr. Lazarus replied, "but to hells to change them into heavens!" After a farewell tour to visit friends and family in Europe, the elderly archimandrite landed safely in Anchorage on December 14, 1989, just

---

7   Published by Anaphora Press (http://anaphorapress.com).

before Mt. Redoubt erupted, spewing ash all over south-central Alaska and closing the airport.

From Diane and Harley's home, Fr. Lazarus continued to write and translate and assist the Eagle River congregation with its conversion into the canonical Orthodox Church. I knew Fr. Lazarus only briefly; ten months after sitting for that snapshot at our February chrismation celebration, he died on November 27, 1992, in his small bedroom at Harley and Diane's. His frail body was placed in a plain wooden coffin in the front room of their home, and friends came and went at all hours, some to pay their respects to a holy man, others to keep the traditional vigil for a priest by taking their turn at reading from the Gospels. I remember the chill breeze that stirred the curtains at the windows, opened wide to aid in preserving Fr. Lazarus's unembalmed body, and the cloth placed over his face during his funeral service, symbol of the hidden life he lived as a monk. He lies buried in the St. John's cemetery, and the large stone cross, donated by a group of his admirers, marks his grave.

Other reminders of Fr. Lazarus linger in the community. When someone sets out on a journey, he is likely to hear a farewell phrase attributed to Fr. Lazarus: "TWA—travel with angels!" Many remember and repeat the words he used when reflecting on his departure from this life: "I want to go up like a bubble that doesn't cause any trouble." And hanging in the living room of the Big House is a large oil portrait of him, painted by Alexei Antonov, a Russian painter whose family also lived for a time at Harley and Diane's. In the picture, the serene monk sits next to a few of the many books he brought with him to Eagle River, holding his copy of the Slavonic Gospel.

Two years ago, Fr. Meletios Webber, an Oxford-educated priest and, like Fr. Lazarus, a convert from Anglicanism, visited St. John's to teach at the Institute. Relating to us his own "Orthodox pedigree," the list of influential men who received him into the Church, Fr. Meletios mentioned Bishop Kallistos Ware and Metropolitan Anthony Bloom. Regarding Fr. Lazarus, Fr. Meletios had this to say: "I never met him, but his renown at Oxford was enormous. . . . He was a man whose light was far too big for his bushel. And I think in the long term it might turn out that he was a very important person in the life of the Church. But for the moment, he still remains somewhat obscure."

Because Fr. Lazarus found his place in the community at St. John's, and because I and my family were welcomed to the same community by Harley and Diane, we were blessed to make the acquaintance of a remarkable man. May his memory, obscure though it may be in this present time, be eternal in the Kingdom that is to come.

IN THE BASEMENT OF MY NEIGHBOR MAYE'S HOUSE IS A TINY apartment, filled with books and photos and memories of a long life. The apartment is home to Fr. John and his faithful dog Teddy and is, God willing, the place where he will stay until he joins his wife Nancy Lee in the cemetery just a short walk from his own door.

Eight years ago, when Fr. John and Khouria Nancy Lee first visited St. John's to lead a marriage enrichment seminar (both were professional counselors in California and they often worked together), Nancy Lee's body and brain were already being destroyed by "progressive supranuclear palsy," a rare disease with no known cause, treatment, or cure, that results in complete disability and death.

During their thirty-year marriage, Fr. John and Nancy Lee were so inseparable that friends often joked they were "joined at the hip." With the onset of Nancy Lee's illness, those words would take on a different, sadder meaning. For three years, Fr. John was her caregiver and watchdog, until her death and burial in California.

Fr. John coped with the new emptiness in his life by working hard and staying busy, both as a counselor and as a priest. But he couldn't work twenty-four hours a day, and everything he saw reminded him of Nancy Lee. He soon knew he would have to leave California, but where could he go? Back to Maryland, the home of his birth and boyhood? He had no family left there, no church, no community. To another country, Latin America perhaps, as a missionary? At his age, the language barrier would be difficult to overcome.

All his life, Fr. John had felt drawn to mountainous places. The first line of a familiar poem frequently came to his mind: "Bring me men to match my mountains." He remembered that visit to Eagle River and the close-knit church community in the shadow of the Chugach Mountains, and he picked up the phone and called Fr. Marc to arrange a one-month visit.

After that month, Fr. John knew he had found his place in the community at St. John's, and he soon moved here to stay. Here, he says, his grief has ceased to be an enemy and has become a means of transformation. Living alone has even become a positive experience, allowing him time and space for prayer and meditation. And he has served the St. John's parish as priest, confessor, and counselor.

As Fr. John's mind and spirit grew calmer, two things became clear. His love for the St. John's community convinced him that this is his place, the spot where he wants to spend the rest of his life and where he wishes to be buried. It was unthinkable that he would not be buried beside Nancy Lee, so he decided to arrange for her body to be reinterred in the St. John's cemetery.

On an overcast summer afternoon, everything was ready, and

several dozen parishioners gathered at the St. John's cemetery to join Fr. John in the prayers for the departed. Once again, Nancy Lee's coffin was lowered into the ground, and there she rests, visited often by friends who, though we missed the chance to know her in this life, are happy that we can remember her along with the others who rest there with her.

Nancy Lee, though she never made this community her home in life, has, like her loving husband, found her place in it.

MANY FOLKS IN OUR COMMUNITY HAVE A STORY ABOUT why coming to the Big House felt like coming home. Seventeen years ago, Bill and I and our sons began our long goodbye to the church of our ancestors, but had not yet made the commitment to Orthodoxy. In the summer of that year, we attended inquirers' classes at the Big House, where we sat on comfy sofas, listened through the open windows to the pleasant drone of a mower on the lawn, and sniffed the fragrance of fresh-cut grass as it drifted in on a light breeze. Like thirsty nomads on our way to a promising new land, we sat in the cool oasis that is the Big House living room and drank in Fr. Marc's teaching.

It was there that we met Nancy and Bob, who had recently moved with their three young children from Florida to live in the community. Bob was a former Presbyterian pastor who, upon announcing to his superiors his intention to pursue a study of Orthodoxy, was presented with a plaque commemorating his immediate defrocking.

On that first Saturday afternoon, they sat across from us—Nancy, dark and intense, and Bob, red-haired and laid-back. He stretched his long legs comfortably in front of him while, for two hours or so, we read and discussed what Bp. Kallistos Ware, himself a convert from Protestantism, said about *The Orthodox Church*.

When the class was over, we headed to our car, and Nancy ran to catch up with us. "I'm interested in your accent," she said in her bold way. "I think we should get to know each other." Ordinarily, Yankee comments about my speech ruffle my feathers, but Nancy's unique invitation to friendship won me over completely.

Next week, we were back in the living room and, seated across from us, smiling and relaxed, were Nancy and Bob. I was horrified to see a pair of crutches beside Bob, and in the place where just six days earlier his left leg had been, there was an empty trouser leg. How was it possible, I thought, that a man could lose a leg and, within a week, appear so completely normal and at ease? And why didn't anyone besides me look worried? Couldn't they see that his leg was *missing*?

I fretted over this strange mystery until we took a break, then I watched Bob grab the crutches and swing off the sofa as easily as an Olympic gymnast executing a perfect flip from the parallel rings. Ordinarily, a polite Southern girl like me wouldn't dream of asking a stranger about his physical disability. But Bob seemed to be a friendly, open guy, and I just had to know the answer.

He laughed at my apologetic question. He lost his leg, he said, in a motorcycle accident when he was 18, on the day of his high school graduation. He stayed in the hospital for a long time; he was fortunate to survive. Sometimes, he said, he wears a prosthetic leg, and some-times he doesn't. It wasn't exactly a cheery explanation, but I figured if he was okay with it, then I would be too.

In just a few years, Bob would be ordained, first a deacon, then a priest, and would from then on be "Fr. Stephen." Every year during the first week of Lent, Bill and I watched him during the long penitential prayers of the Canon of St. Andrew. The prayers call for dozens of full-body prostrations, and we creaked and panted our way through them while Fr. Stephen executed them nimbly, without breaking a sweat. And when we asked him why he, of all people, had no handicapped tag on his minivan, he shrugged and said uninterestedly, "Never needed one."

Anyway, back then, during our four-month catechumenate, our oldest sons were teenagers and our youngest was four. During that time, we tried our best to absorb everything from sacraments to infant baptism to confession. Bred from generations of Baptists, I knew that baptizing babies was the province of superstitious papists and haughty Episcopalians, not plain, Bible-believing Christians like us. When I walked down the church aisle at age nine and told the preacher I wanted to be baptized, I did what every good Baptist was expected to do. I made my own decision to accept Christ as my personal Lord and Savior. I "got saved."

The Orthodox Church recognizes prior baptisms done in the name of the Trinity, so my husband, myself, and our two older sons were okay—we had been immersed in the name of the Father, Son, and Holy Spirit. But our four-year-old had not made his decision; we would have to make it for him. Now, I could deal with that idea *in theory*, but the reality was scary. Who were we, I thought, to "direct" a child into the waters of baptism? Fortunately, my husband was well informed on this question, and after we read up on the matter and talked it over at length, my mind was set at rest.

The day before our scheduled chrismation, our fifteen-year-old told us he wasn't ready and he still had questions that needed answers. Alarmed and not wishing to force our children into anything for which they were not prepared, we asked him to tell us his concern.

His questions were those that many converts stumble over on their way to Orthodoxy: Does the Church worship Mary? Why do we ask her to "save" us? Do I have to pray to her?

An acceptance of Mary and her place in the theology and ritual of the Orthodox Church often takes time for Protestant converts to acquire. I have found that it is a process of assimilation, that moments of understanding are often followed by more questions, by unsettling moments of skepticism, and even by doubt and fear.

It was at the Third Ecumenical Council in AD 431 that St. Cyril of Alexandria and the other Fathers of the Church affirmed the use of the term *Theotokos*, a Greek word meaning "God-bearer," to describe Mary. At that time, dissenters within the Church argued that a more accurate name for her is *Christotokos*, as the one she bore is the Son of God, not God Himself. The Fathers realized, of course, that to accede to this argument was to announce that Christ was not God, that He was not, at the same time, fully man and fully divine. And that was unthinkable.

Orthodox Christians worship God only, but we honor and pray to Mary. Why? Because to do so is in line with biblical example. The angel Gabriel, Mary's cousin Elizabeth, Jesus, and even God Himself honored her. She is called, by Elizabeth, the "Mother of my Lord."

Jesus' first public miracle was done at her request, when she asked Him to help the poor servants who had run out of wine for the wedding. Instead of backing away apologetically when Jesus seemed to brush her off, Mary stood her ground and told the servants, "Whatever He says to you, do it." That is why it's good to ask for her help; her intercession is powerful. (Of course, first you have to get over the hang-up about talking to a person who is no longer living on earth, but that is another story.)

A PLACE TO REST

In my reading, I found these words helpful:

[I]t is the integrity of her [Mary's] faith which for Jesus is the greatness of His mother. The Mother of God by the consent of her faith had a unique vocation which is described as a "sword that will pierce her soul." Mary is the figure of the true disciple, the model of the demanding *sequela Christi*, the following after Christ, to which every person, man and woman, is called.[8]

Our son, as I said, needed answers immediately, and without hesitating, we telephoned Fr. Marc and drove to his house (we still lived in Anchorage then) for an emergency catechumen class. Adam was reassured, and we—I, my husband, and our two older sons—were chrismated the next day. Our youngest was happily baptized, and since then I have come to understand the Orthodox belief that salvation is a journey that does not end with baptism. That is just the beginning.

An Eastern Christian does not approach God as an isolated individual; he worships Him as a member of the Body of Christ. His supplications do not rise up like the voice of a solo singer, they form part of a great choir in which all the Saints and all the sinners have their share. Among all these voices there is one that sounds more distinctly than any other, for it is the voice of the purest and the holiest, the most humble and the most loving of all human beings; the Mother of Jesus Christ. She, the Mother of God, is also the Mother of all men and women; for no one can be a stranger to her who gave birth to the Savior of the whole world.

—NICHOLAS ZERNOV,

A MANUAL OF EASTERN ORTHODOX PRAYERS

---

8   Elisabeth Behr-Sigel, *Discerning the Signs of the Times*, St. Vladimir's Seminary Press, 2001, p. 110.

GIFTS FROM A WISE MAN

DECEMBER

FEAST OF THE NATIVITY OF THE LORD

Your Nativity, O Christ our God, has shown to us the light of knowledge;
for by it those who adored the stars, through a star were taught to worship
You, O Son of Righteousness, and to know You, the Dayspring from on
high. O Lord, glory to You.

—TROPARION OF THE FEAST

JUST BEFORE CHRISTMAS I WAS IN THE CHECKOUT LINE AT one of Eagle River's big box stores when I saw a tall, familiar-looking man in a nearby aisle, hands behind his back, studying the covers at the magazine rack. He was dressed all in black, from his head to his toes. His eyes, behind gold wire-rimmed glasses, were kind and alert, and his beard was short and neatly trimmed. Plugged in his ear was a blinking Bluetooth cell phone.

The man I saw is the overseer of St. John's church and shepherd of its flock, our Bishop Joseph, who had traveled from his home in Los Angeles for his annual Christmas visit to Eagle River. Was he doing some last-minute shopping of his own, I wondered, and what did bishops shop for, anyway? He seemed so out of place in the crowded store that I felt awkward about greeting him there. I toyed with the idea of paying for my purchases, ducking my head, and hurrying out the door.

That's when I saw a couple of my St. John's neighbors, who also happened to be in the store, rushing excitedly to the magazine rack. How could I ignore my bishop, no matter what unexpected place he turned up in? So I headed his way to join the welcoming committee.

The traditional way to greet a bishop is to approach him with hands outstretched, palms turned upward and held together, one on top of the other. This gesture is accompanied by a slight bow and a spoken greeting, usually, "Hello, Your Grace." By the time I got it all together and was ready to say hello, Bishop Joseph was smiling and putting his arms around me, sweeping away all my awkward shyness with a completely unselfconscious hug.

Every Christmas, the community at St. John's is visited by a wise man who brings us gifts of love, encouragement, and instruction. Bishop Joseph Al-Zehlaoui was born in Damascus, Syria, and educated there and at Our Lady of Balamand Monastery in Koura, Northern Lebanon. In 1995 he was selected to be an auxiliary bishop for the Antiochian Orthodox Christian Archdiocese of North America and assigned to the western United States, with his headquarters at Los Angeles.

Bishop Joseph's early visits to us were a bit challenging (for us, not for him). We were charmed by his accent and his occasional search for just the right word, but on the flip side, we sometimes had difficulty understanding exactly what he wanted to communicate to us. Over time, the language gaps have narrowed considerably, and he speaks to us with ease on any subject.

When he first began to make his annual visit to Alaska, he says that he was often asked, "Are you crazy to go to Alaska during the cold and freezing time of the year?" And he answered, "Yes, I am crazy!" Although his chief duty is to serve and pastor his clergy, Bishop Joseph's affection for all of us is obvious and endearing.

If you ever have a chance to attend an Orthodox Divine Liturgy when a bishop is the main celebrant, I suggest that you do it. If your preferred style of worship leans toward minimalism, be prepared for a sensory feast. The ordinary pageantry of the Church is kicked up a few notches when the bishop is present, and the service is marked by much bowing of the clergy in the bishop's direction and kissing of his hand. He is addressed as "Master," and if he is like our Bishop Joseph, he will not hesitate to firmly correct a deacon, priest, or acolyte who makes a misstep. He even wears a jewel-encrusted miter that anyone can plainly see is really a crown.

We Orthodox call the bishop our *hierarch* (chief priest), and the government of the Church is a *hierarchy*, that is, a system of offices ranked in order from highest to lowest. It is this ranking system, along with the levels of authority that go with it, that nettles many an independent Protestant, and, come to think of it, many a Catholic and Orthodox as well. But my experience tells me that the imposition of order and authority, tempered by love and respect for each other, is a tricky balance to maintain in any community of Christians.

In fact, I learned that the concept of *authority* has a bit of contentious history in our own community. But it is an instructive history because it reveals that life here is not and never has been a carefree bed of roses, that living and worshipping together requires a willingness to trust, to forgive, to deal with change, and to keep going forward together.

Back when Grace Community Church, as the group then called itself, was moving toward Orthodox worship and theology, dissension occasionally arose—naturally enough, given the rejection of traditional religion that brought the people together in the first place. The organization of leadership by elders, priests, and deacons, the wearing of special clothing by the clergy, the changes in worship—all these were sometimes difficult for everyone to accept at the same time. But the thorniest change of all was the idea of submission to authority.

The Grace Community published a tract stating that it placed a high priority on commitment to true community and to authoritative leadership. Christians are meant to be "truly involved in each others' lives," the tract said, while being "committed and submitted to their leaders." The intent was to make sure that everyone was covered by pastoral care, a good thing. The not-so-good part was the anger and embarrassment that sometimes resulted from the "disciplining" of individuals. For years, according to some who have been here a long time, it was believed that no one should act on an important personal decision without first receiving a "blessing" from the priest.

But it was not so much the imposition of discipline that chipped at the cohesion of the community. It was rather objections to the direction in which Harold Dunaway was leading the community—that is, toward Orthodoxy—that really shook things up. Some believed that in the old Big House days, they had been on the right path, and that a wonderful community was forming. In their view, all this had been spoiled by the influence of Peter Gillquist and his group with their unwelcome innovations. The church archives reveal that one man, described as an "aggressive divider," was asked to leave, and that two others, who vocally sympathized with him, left of their own accord.

To make matters worse, a couple of the dissenters joined the

Bethany Baptist Church in Anchorage, a church of free spirits that described itself as "leaderless" and which already included outspoken critics of Harold Dunaway and Grace Community Church. Unfortunately, some close friendships had been damaged by Grace Community's move toward formal, structured worship.

Fr. Harold acknowledges that there was some heavy-handedness in the imposition of authority back in those days, that maybe they even went way overboard. But he also believes that "we would not be where we are today if it had not been done." In other words, the mistakes we make in the past often prepare us for growth and understanding in the future.

To try to ease some of the tension between Grace Community Church and its detractors at Bethany Baptist Church, a meeting took place over thirty years ago for which Fr. Marc wrote an introduction. It is preserved in the church archives, and his words, I believe, are still true of the St. John's church community today:

> The people in our congregation are simply a people who desire nothing more in all the world than to know the will of God and live holy lives in submission to Him. We were this same people many years ago when we were nothing but a group of Christians meeting in homes, excited about the grace of God. . . . We knew then that God had truly spoken to us about the issue of His grace and forgiveness and we were sold out to this truth. But there were some very important things about God's truth that we lacked during that time, so God, in His constant provision, began to reveal these things to us. And in His wisdom, He chose to do this through the very same men who had given us our start in knowing the grace of God. From them we heard things that they felt God was teaching them, and we became convicted, for we witnessed that this was indeed the truth and the will of God for us.

"Unity without the divine presence," said Matthew the Poor, "is nothing more than an idea, a matter for discussion, or a vain longing. But in the presence of God, unity becomes real and visible, overflowing and life-giving, and many live it. When Christ is present in the midst of a community in conflict, controversy cannot keep from ceasing. Every member must begin to fill his eyes and his heart with true unity, and prepare his whole being to receive unity and to give it."[9]

THIS IS A GOOD PLACE TO FINISH TELLING THE STORY OF our son Adam's illness and treatment. But first, I must go back farther, to the days when we were newly Orthodox and decided to visit a monastery that advertised a miracle-working weeping icon. We were skeptical of some of the "foreign" trappings of Orthodoxy, but we were on vacation and the monastery was on a lovely mountaintop, so we went.

The monks welcomed us and gave us a tour of the grounds and buildings, followed by prayer before the icon. When my turn came to venerate it, I was prepared to scoff, but standing before it, almost against my will, I prayed for healing of a minor ailment that had annoyed me for many years. Even though I felt emotionally touched, I was not at all prepared to expect any "miracle."

Talking it over in the car afterward, we agreed that, though we still had our doubts and questions, we were willing to concede that there might be something special about those monks, something the world found easy to scorn and even to persecute. For my part, the

---

9   Matthew the Poor, *The Communion of Love*, St. Vladimir's Seminary Press, 1984, p. 229.

visit left me with a sense of well-being and peace, and from that day to this, I have been entirely free of the ailment from which I asked to be healed.

Three years later, we returned to the mountaintop monastery to pray for Adam, who would soon undergo surgery. The monks not only prayed with us and anointed Adam with the tears of the weeping icon, but also visited him at the hospital. And here is where the subject of submission and authority comes in. As we greeted each monk respectfully, as we had been taught, with a kiss on his hand, we were watched by my mother, a passionate skeptic. "How can you do that?" she demanded to know. "What makes them so special?"

I could only explain that, in kissing the hand of a monk or a priest, the honor being shown passes to God, the One represented by His clergy on earth, the men who stand and serve in His name. My mother, though polite and even grudgingly friendly to our monk visitors, was not convinced. Authority, she believes, belongs to God alone, and so does our submission.

On the day of surgery, we waited for eight hours while Dr. Grossman and his team worked to extricate the tumor from our son's brain. When the doctor came out to us in the waiting room, he assured us that Adam had come through the surgery just fine, and that he was confident the tumor had been entirely removed. However, he said, as a precaution, Adam would need to be treated with both radiation and chemotherapy.

Our gratitude and relief on hearing that the surgery had gone well turned at once into the creeping fear that seems always to follow the word "chemotherapy." All we could do was watch over Adam while he recovered in the ICU for three days, wait for the pathology lab results, and pray. We were humbled and awed to learn later that, through an

Orthodox prayer chain, Christians all over the world were praying for our son.

On the third day, we ran into Dr. Grossman in the hospital hall, and he greeted us with these words: "It looks as if you have received your miracle. Everything is fine. There won't be any need for further treatment." Though we had not talked to him about it, he too had learned about the prayers. Our story, thanks be to God, had a blessed ending.

The story of the monks who prayed with us, however, turned out to be an ugly, sad one. They were quick to spread the news that the tears of their weeping icon had brought about a miracle. Unfortunately, some years later, they admitted that, among other crimes, they had conspired to defraud by causing their beautiful icon to shed phony tears. The details are not necessary; it is enough to say that they broke the laws of man and God and sentence has been passed on them by the civil government. My mother's suspicions were justified—these men were in no way worthy of the respect and honor that was given to them.

And yet . . . we prayed with them and Adam experienced healing.

It seems inevitable that we will sometimes place our trust in those who are not deserving of it. And it is sad and destructive when we allow our faith in God to be shaken by unworthy spiritual leaders. But it is not they to whom we pray. It is God who "forgives all your iniquities, who heals all your diseases." The healing experienced by my son was not a reward for our piety, nor was it evidence of the holiness of the men with whom we prayed. Adam's healing was a sign of God's mercy and a reminder that faith is the only essential requirement for Him to act in our lives. St. James reminds us that "the prayer of faith will save the sick, and the Lord will raise him up."

What should I say to my skeptical mother and to all who question the worthiness of spiritual guides and leaders to whom we Orthodox show honor? The only thing I *can* say is that all of us—victorious saints and ordinary survivors alike—will be required to answer for what we have done, based on the light that has been given to each of us. The rest is up to God.

FORTUNATELY, THE CHURCH CAN BOAST OF MANY MEN AND women who *are* worthy of veneration. This group includes the apostles, martyrs, forefathers, patriarchs, prophets, and ascetics—in other words, the saints. Among the saints is a Russian missionary to Alaska who spent much of his life here, serving the Church, the Alaskan Native people, and the Russian colonizers who ruled over them. As a teenager in Moscow, he had chosen the ascetic life of a monk. His name was Herman.

Over two hundred years ago, while European settlers in the American colonies were mobilizing for revolution, a small party of Christian missionaries landed at Kodiak in the future state of Alaska. They were sent there by the Church in Russia and charged with aiding and evangelizing the Native people they encountered. Among them was the Monk Herman, who, on the surface at least, appeared to possess none of the qualifications for this work. He was not an ordained minister; in fact, he had no formal education at all. He had no particular skills, humanly speaking, which would mark him as a man of talent and promise. The only traits he had to recommend him were his goodness, his faith, and his practice of continuous prayer.

These, it turned out, were all he needed. He became, in his own words, the "humble servant and nurse" of the Native people of Alaska, their teacher, spiritual father, and defender. Tirelessly, he labored on their behalf, defending them against the cruelty of the Russian traders, pleading their cause before the Russian rulers, and caring for their orphaned children.

He lived in a beautiful green forest on Spruce Island. On the island were three small wooden buildings—a hut, a chapel, and a combined school and guest house. This was Father Herman's home for more than forty years and where, on December 13, 1837, he died.

It is because of those first Orthodox missionaries that Alaska today is studded with domed, quaintly picturesque churches. They are much more than tourist attractions; they and the people who worship in them are those Russian missionaries' living legacy. Today, the simple monk Herman is revered by millions as Saint Herman of Alaska, and the world celebrates his memory on December 13. His adopted people, we Americans, are particularly fortunate to remember him and his simplicity so near to Christmas, that American season of consumerism and indulgence.

By the standards of even some so-called "religious leaders," who preach the gospel of power, possessions, and pleasure, St. Herman was a miserable failure. He lived and died in obscurity among humble people. He left behind no material wealth, no great books, no portraits or statues of his physical likeness. But the name of St. Herman of Alaska—the "North Star of Christ's Holy Church"—will be forever remembered by Christians throughout the world.

IT WAS ST. HERMAN WHO BROUGHT STEVEN, THE TALENTED Native American musician, and his family to live in Alaska. Just before St. Herman's December feast day, I catch sight of Steven, dressed in jeans and cowboy boots, dashing from his home on Monastery Drive to one of his many business and artistic commitments. And I wonder: Does he ever feel conflicted about his identity? Did he ever have to rediscover his culture? Or did he never misplace it? And how does his Orthodox Christian identity get along with his Native American identity? Are these idiotic questions? I decided to ask him.

Born of Native American and Hispanic parents, Steven was an Air Force kid whose earliest memories include living in Okinawa and Hawaii, serving as an altar boy in the Roman Catholic Church, and saying his prayers every night. Even as a child, he had a strong faith in God.

His family was a traditional, sit-down-to-dinner-together unit. Sundays, he recalls, always started with Mass, then lunch at the NCO club, followed by fun at the beach. His two older brothers were altar boys before him, and he loved the vividness of the red and white cassocks and surplices that they wore on high holy days.

Steven's dad was raised by his grandmother until the federal government stepped in and placed him in a boarding school, where his ethnic culture was pretty much suppressed. He was, Steven says, a "boarding school casualty." Now deceased, his dad never talked much about those days.

After his dad's retirement, the family moved to the Bay Area of California. Steven was fifteen years old, and it was then that he began to lose interest in the Mass, while at the same time he became more interested in reading the Bible. Most of his friends were born-again believers, and by the time he was a senior in high school, he realized the Catholic Church was no longer "doing it" for him.

After graduation, he attended a Nazarene church, where he directed the youth choir. At that church, he says, it was all about the altar call and experiencing a transformation. He felt no need to respond to the altar call, and he never was aware of being transformed, so he began to wonder if there was something wrong with him. He finally did respond to an altar call, not to be "saved," but to publicly dedicate his musical gifts to God.

Steven attended college at San Jose State, where he studied music. He got married while in college and, after graduation, worked as a music teacher at a Christian school and directed music at an Assembly of God church. His wife grew up in a non-churchgoing, alcoholic family, and Steven, who had learned from his own loving parents to find strength through faith, struggled to understand his wife's experience as a child of alcoholics. The marriage ended when their daughter was five. The Assembly of God is not too sympathetic with divorce, especially when it involves their leaders, so Steven moved to the newly formed Vineyard Christian Fellowship, where he later became the music director.

Steven told me that he did experience a loss of connection with his Native American heritage. During his college years, with the help and encouragement of a Native American buddy, he started to reconnect. But it was not until after the breakup of his marriage that his reconnection took a new and dramatic direction. He participated in two ancient rituals of the Native American people, the sweat lodge and the vision quest. Those experiences would culminate in his being given a new, and very significant, name.

The *inipi,* the sacred sweat lodge ceremony of the Lakota Sioux, is believed to cleanse the body, mind, and soul, while preparing the participant to receive divine intervention. The *inipi* is a community event and is not undertaken alone. The sweat lodge, built in the shape of a round dome, represents the universe. Centered inside the sweat lodge is the fireplace, the center of the universe. Large stones, which have been heated outside the lodge, are placed in the fireplace, and water is poured over them. The entrance is covered, plunging the lodge into steaming darkness. The fragrance of burning sage and cedar permeates the blazing air.

Before entering the *inipi,* participants may have fasted from food for a period of time, a practice that heightens spiritual awareness during the ritual. The lodge leader smudges their faces with sage or cedar and they sit, close together, around the red-hot rocks. For the next four or five hours, more hot rocks are added, and the participants endure the steamy heat while singing traditional songs and prayers. Prayers are divided into four rounds: prayers for yourself; prayers for others; prayers for healing; and prayers of gratitude.

The *inipi* prepared Steven for his next spiritual endeavor, the *hanblecheyapi,* the "vision quest" of the traditional Lakota culture. It is a rite of passage, a journey alone into the wilderness to seek personal growth and spiritual guidance. To seek a vision is to seek an inner revelation that grants meaning and direction to one's life. Traditionally, a medicine man acts as the seeker's guide through the vision quest and is responsible for interpreting the vision.

For four days and nights, taking with him only a blanket, Steven remained alone in a wilderness area in Oregon and fasted from food and water. In the wilderness, he had a dream: He was running, very fast, through a forest, jumping over rocks and bushes as if on four legs. In a clearing, he came upon a deer lying on the ground. He stopped to look at the deer, and the deer spoke to him. "I am wounded. Help our people," it said. The deer looked down, and then up, and this time it appeared older. It said again, "I am wounded. Help our people." Once more, the deer looked down, then up, and this time it appeared close to death. For the third time, it spoke. "I am wounded. Help our people." Then Steven woke up.

He shared his vision with the medicine man, who knew that Steven was a Christian. And the medicine man interpreted the dream: The deer, he said, represents the Native American people. The deer spoke three times, not four (four is a number sacred to Native Americans). Steven's dream, the medicine man concluded, meant that he must somehow find a way to bridge the gap between the two worlds, that of the Christians and that of the Native people. From that time, Steven would be called Wounded Deer. The dream, and the name, would take on even greater significance in the years to come.

Despite his divorce and departure from the Assembly of God school, Steven remained close to his old boss, the principal, and to his boss's family. Jennifer, the principal's daughter, was a good friend, and eventually, Steven asked for and received permission from her dad to court her. In due time, he and Jennifer were married.

After their wedding, Steven and Jennifer, along with a missionary team from the Vineyard church, traveled to Romania to do mission work. One day, Steven performed with a group of Vineyard singers in Cluj, the capital of Transylvania. He remembers that they stood in front of the statue of a medieval king who led his people to turn back the invasion of the Muslims.

As his group sang, Steven saw two Orthodox priests, dressed in their long, black cassocks, deep in conversation as they walked together. He was curious, but had no clue who they were or what church they represented. He only knew that they paid no attention to the group of American Protestant singers on the street.

The Vineyard church had about three hundred members and was doing well. When the pastor asked him to take over as worship leader,

Steven was ecstatic. He is a rock-and-roll musician by profession, and he was being given the opportunity to do what he loved, and to do it in church. *This*, he thought, *is as good as it gets.*

In time, though, the Vineyard congregation began to ask, What next? Together, for forty days, they prayed and fasted and sought direction from God. During this time, Steven's pastor listened as a colleague told him excitedly about a different church, the Orthodox Church. *He must be crazy,* the pastor thought, but he went on listening and began to change his mind. At the end of the forty days, he believed God was leading the Vineyard people to Orthodoxy, but he had no idea how to take them there. Then he had a revelation: God would handle it, not he.

As it worked out, sixty-five percent of the Vineyard members opted out of conversion, and the rest, including Steven and Jennifer, were chrismated six months later. At the same time, Steven was ordained to the office of subdeacon and soon realized that the significance of his name—Wounded Deer, the one who would help bridge the gap between Christianity and his people—was coming into sharper focus. His work with Orthodox music taught him much about church theology, and the more he learned, the more parallels he saw between Native American spirituality and Orthodoxy.

Meanwhile, Steven continued on the journey of rediscovery of his ethnic heritage. He decided to participate in the most significant religious ceremony of the North American Plains Indians, the Sundance. The Sundance is a ritual that takes place during a traditional spring gathering of Native American tribes, during which the participants reaffirm their belief in the renewal of the earth and everything in it. The Sundance is not to be undertaken lightly. Steven spent four years in preparation before traveling back to Oregon, where the intertribal ceremony would take place under the direction of a trusted medicine man.

First, the sun dancers fasted from food for four days while they created the traditional "tobacco ties" (small pouches of colored cloth filled with tobacco that represent the Sundancer's prayers). On the Sundance site, they built the "arbor," a circle of trees covered with cedar branches. (The ceremony takes place within the arbor; singers and family members watch from outside the arbor and offer prayers of support.) Together, the dancers chose a special tree, cut it down, and carried it to the center of the arbor, being careful that the tree did not touch the ground until it was placed upright in the center of the arbor. In this way, the tree retained the strength and life force it had been given by the Creator.

Before midnight of the first day, the Sundancers entered the arbor and began their fast from both food and water, a fast that would last for the next four days. After the *inipi* ritual at sunrise, they filled their ceremonial pipes with *kinnickinnick*, the bark of the red willow tree, and tobacco, and plugged the pipes with sage. They put on the traditional Sundance skirts and eagle bone whistles, placed two eagle feathers in their headbands, and began the dance "rounds" that lasted throughout the day. Some dancers chose to undergo the traditional body piercings; others did not.

Steven told me that after participating in the Sundance, a man is called *warrior*, and his job is to serve and protect his people. The warrior's calling, he noticed, is similar to that of an Orthodox deacon. A warrior puts the will and the needs of his people ahead of his own.

Steven read with amazement the lives of three Alaskan saints: the missionary monk Herman, who taught Christianity to the Native peoples of Alaska without quashing their culture, and who was loved and revered by them; Juvenaly, the martyred heiromonk (priest/monk) who defied a shaman's order to stop preaching and was killed in a hail of arrows; and Peter the Aleut, the Native boy who was taken captive by Spanish soldiers and killed when he refused to accept their Catholic religion. And Steven thought: *This is something the Native American people can really hold on to.*

During the year that Steven and two of his friends turned forty, they decided to mark the occasion with a pilgrimage to Kodiak, Alaska, where they would pray at the grave of St. Herman. Steven prayed that he would be allowed and empowered to serve the Native American people as St. Herman did. On their way back to California, the men stopped off in Eagle River to visit St. John's. Steven stayed in the guest room at the Big House and met Fr. Marc and Fr. Harold, whom he "loved right away."

As it turned out, that journey to the grave of St. Herman was the starting point for another one, a move that would bring him to live in a place where his prayer could begin to be answered. He heard of a job opportunity in Anchorage, landed the job, and less than a year after his prayer at the grave of St. Herman, Steven, Jennifer, and their children moved to Alaska. They found their place in the community at St. John's, and Steven's work allows him to serve the Alaskan Native people, with whom he feels more than a connection of kinship.

During Anchorage's midwinter "Fur Rendezvous" celebration, Steven and Medicine Dream performed downtown, and Robin and I joined the crowd at the civic center to hear them. We listened to a couple of songs, but it was hot inside the big meeting room. As we started to leave, Paul, the lead singer, announced a "Friendship Dance." While the drums pounded, people went to the dance floor and formed a circle. Moving clockwise, they danced and swayed in time with the music while others—men, women, boys, girls, old, and young, mostly Native Americans—drifted out to join them.

Then the moving circle divided itself into two, a circle within a circle, and the one inside began to turn in a counterclockwise direction. The dancers faced each other, and as they met, they smiled, shook hands, and greeted one another. I whispered to Robin, "It looks like our forgiveness circle."

Her eyes widened, she looked at me and said, "Let's go get in it!"

"Oh no," I said, drawing back as she reached for my hand. I could never do that. My timidity, my apprehension at leaving the safety of my comfort zone would not allow it.

"Come on!" Robin headed for the dance floor. Then, before I could change my mind, I followed her. We squeezed into one of the circles and began to smile and shake hands, and suddenly, I was no longer a watcher. In a small, barely noticed way, I was *part* of them. For a few minutes, I had found a place in their world.

Thank you, Steven, for helping me to put a tentative foot on the bridge that God and St. Herman have called you to build for your people.

From this day, this hour, this very moment, we should strive to love God above all else and do His will.

—ST. HERMAN OF ALASKA

Let us begin this very day, this very hour, the Great Healing to come. Let us walk the Red Road in Peace.

—LAKOTA PRAYER

BELONGERS

JANUARY

FEAST OF THEOPHANY

*When You were baptized in the Jordan, O Lord, the worship of the Trinity
was made manifest. And the voice of the Father bore witness to You, calling You Beloved Son. And the Spirit, in the form of a dove, confirmed the
truthfulness of His word. O Christ our God, who have revealed Yourself
and enlightened the world, glory to You.*

—TROPARION OF THE FEAST

THE LIVING ROOM LOOKS ORDINARY AGAIN WITHOUT THE
Christmas tree, and my precious collection of ornaments—many of
which are the boys' faded and tattered childhood handiwork—is back
on the closet shelf. The twelve days of Christmas have passed and I,
along with most of my neighbors, am cleaning house in preparation
for a house-blessing visit from Fr. Marc.

After a December drought, serious snow began falling on Christmas
Eve and never stopped. We are living in a wonderland of brief white
days and long, silvery nights. It is so cold that the inside of my micro-
wave oven, vented to the outside, is coated with a layer of frost.

171

Axel needs exercise this evening, so, even though my chores have left me longing for the comfort of my warm sofa, I bundle up, hitch him to the leash, and brace myself to open the door. In the silent darkness, we follow our familiar path up Monastery Drive to the highway intersection, then turn around to walk the short distance to the cathedral.

The streetlight at the end of our driveway spills a soft golden glow onto the snow piled on either side of the road, and the tree branches, heavy with snow, droop overhead, giving the empty road an arched, cavernous look. It looks like the streetlight in Narnia where Lucy met Mr. Tumnus, when it was "always winter and never Christmas," before Aslan destroyed the power of the White Witch and caused the frozen landscape to melt into rushing rivers and sparkling lakes.

Water, frozen and unfrozen, is practically synonymous with Alaska. Clear, rocky rivers, lacy waterfalls, blue-white icebergs floating in glacial lakes—pictures of these are the stuff of the tourist's dreams as he pores longingly over the cruise brochure or the article about the wilderness fishing lodge.

Theophany[10] is the feast that features water in a prominent role. Theophany celebrates the revelation of Christ as the Son of God, announced by the descent of the dove as He was baptized in the Jordan River by His cousin John. The Liturgy of Theophany features a long prayer before the font, during which Fr. Marc plunges the gold blessing cross three times into the water, transforming it, in a *mystery,* into the holy water that will be used later to bless the cathedral and our homes, to bless the palms and branches on the next Palm Sunday,

---

10   In the Western Church, the Feast of Theophany is better known as Epiphany, the commemoration of the visit of the Magi to the Christ Child.

and on many other occasions that call for a special blessing. When the Liturgy is over, the deacons will fill pitchers with the blessed water, and we will drink it after we receive communion. We will fill our bottles with it and take it to our homes for use throughout the year.

Every January, after the blessing of the water, Fr. Marc comes to our house, bringing his stole, his blessing brush and bowl, candles, and a service book. We stand with him before the icons in the corner, and he says the prayers of blessing for the house and everyone who lives in it. Then, taking the container of holy water and the sprinkling brush, he walks through each room in the house, flinging water at the walls, the furniture, the pets, and the people. Holding lighted candles, we follow him, singing the hymn of Theophany as we go.

If asked by one of my dear Protestant friends to show her where the Bible mentions house blessings, I would probably say something like this: I know, of course, that the Bible does not spell out the approved procedure for the blessing of houses, or, for that matter, the blessing of anything else. The lighting of a candle, the saying of a prayer special to the occasion, the sprinkling of water—all of these small rituals are examples of the Orthodox way of using ordinary things to sanctify (to *set apart*) everyday life.

And I would hope I could help her understand.

LAST WINTER, BILL AND I VACATIONED IN THE CARIBBEAN, on the Turks and Caicos Islands. Bill had dreamed for years of visiting the TCI, a former British possession that was a haven for displaced British loyalists after the American Revolution. The Tories took their slaves with them to the West Indies and established sugar plantations, but few of the refugees stuck it out for the long haul. Many departed and left their slaves behind, but the abandoned slaves thrived and are now establishing their country as a major tourist destination. Lucky for us, though, the islands are still uncrowded and unspoiled.

When we landed at Providenciales, the largest city, we walked off the plane on one of those portable metal ramps, wearing sunglasses to shield our Alaskan eyes from the intense glare and wishing we had spent more time taking our pale bodies to the tanning salon. In the terminal, I saw three signs directing travelers to the appropriate customs line. The first read "Visitors," the second, "Residents," and the third, "Belongers."

We were met by Alveda, the hotel manager, and as soon as we were in her van, I asked her to tell me about "residents" and "belongers" ("visitors" I could understand). A resident, she said, may have lived in the Turks and Caicos for a very long time, and perhaps will even die there. But a belonger, she said, was born in the islands. His people were born and lived in the islands. The islands are his place. He may go to visit other places; he may even live in other places. But the islands will always be the one place where he *belongs.* "I am a belonger," Alveda said simply.

I envied her the sureness with which she spoke. All humans want to be loved, to be accepted, to belong. Years ago, during a conversation with someone who lived in the St. John's community for a very long time, we talked about the status of early arrivers compared with those who come later. This fellow said that since he didn't know my history, he found it hard to relate to me. He implied that since I had not shared in his history, I could not hope to really know him. At first I was so taken aback that I was speechless. I always seem to need time in such situations to mull over my response. After years of thinking about what he said, I believe Jesus had a better answer than anything I could ever think up.

Remember His story about the owner of a vineyard who needed to hire some help? He went out early one morning and found some guys standing around, so he put them to work with the promise of a denarius at the end of the day. Later that morning, he went back to the marketplace and found some others who had drifted in and were sitting there idly, so he offered them the same deal and put them to work. Twice more that day, he did the same thing, before hiring the last workers at the eleventh hour.

That night, he called the workers in to receive their pay, beginning with the last ones that went to work. The eleventh hour fellows received one denarius for their labor. The worn-out blokes who went to work at dawn received one denarius for their labor. The owner explained to his workers that he reserved the right to treat them in the way he deemed best.

We at St. John's are like those vineyard workers. Some of us got here bright and early, while others overslept and wandered in a little later; a few of us didn't hear there was work available until the middle of the afternoon; and a bunch of us were finishing up other jobs before we went down to the hiring hall. But what is important is that we are all here now, there is always room for others to join us, and there is plenty of work left to do.

Tom and JoAnn, for example, got here bright and early. In 1968, after Tom's tour of duty to Vietnam, they were posted to Ft. Richardson in Anchorage. With their two kids, Tom's mother Grammy Phyl, and a poodle, they drove up the Alcan Highway to Alaska.

JoAnn had become acquainted with Campus Crusade for Christ while Tom was overseas. In Anchorage they met Harold and Barbara

Dunaway and became fast friends, and part of the community that was forming at the Dunaway home. The years passed, and JoAnn and Tom's family grew to include five grandchildren (Grammy Phyl's great-grandchildren).

On April 1, 1987, the day that St. John's became part of the world-wide Orthodox Church, four generations of this family were chrismated together. Since then, Grammy Phyl has passed away, and Tom and JoAnn have welcomed four great-grandchildren of their own to the clan. After the army took them all over the world, they now live contentedly next door to their great-grandchildren. JoAnn feels blessed to watch her family grow, to bake cookies with two little great-granddaughters, to cuddle a new great-grandson, and to see most of her family around her dinner table on special occasions.

Five generations of the same family have worshipped at St. John's, which is quite a feat anywhere, and a notable one in our transient state. But Tom and JoAnn do not believe their family is bound together primarily by ties of blood and location, but rather by worshipping God together and seeking His will for their lives. He has blessed them by leading them to His Church, and giving them a loving family that is committed to Him and to each other.

In our postmodern, fragmented age, it is plain that people—whether surrounded by friends and family or utterly alone—are not only searching for truth, but are also hungry for connection—spiritual and physical—with other humans. The unbelievers, the disaffected, the marginal, the lonely, the afflicted, and the comfortable—these words describe many of us at St. John's who have found in Orthodox Christianity, and in our community, a place to learn, to work, to grow, to contend with ourselves and each other, and to belong.

I cannot leave off writing these stories without assuring you that we in Eagle River do not live in a heaven on earth, but only, as Barbara Dunaway says, in an outpost of the Kingdom. Being here does not mean that we have *arrived*, only that we have been blessed to find others with whom to make the journey. A sense of triumphalism or complacency is out of place in any church or community.

Neither are we all belongers, at least not as my friend Alveda understood the word. Few of us were born into the Orthodox Church or into the community at St. John's, but no matter where we started out and no matter where we live now, we are, nevertheless, belongers. In the Church and in this community of believers, we have found our place.

Let not your heart be troubled; you believe in God, believe also in Me. In my Father's house are many mansions; if it were not so, I would have told you. I go to prepare a place for you. And if I go and prepare a place for you, I will come again and receive you to Myself; that where I am, there you may be also, and where I go you know, and the way you know.

—JOHN 14:1–4

READING LIST

SOME OF OUR FAVORITE BOOKS

Gillquist, Fr. Peter. *Becoming Orthodox* (Conciliar Press, 3rd ed. 2010)

Lewis, C. S. *Mere Christianity* (Granite Publishers, Inc., paperback ed. 2006)

Mathewes-Green, Frederica. *At the Corner of East and Now: A Modern Life in Ancient Christian Orthodoxy* (Conciliar Press, 2nd ed. 2009)

_____. *Facing East: A Pilgrim's Journey into the Mystery of Orthodoxy* (Harper San Francisco, 1997)

Nouwen, Henri. *Behold the Beauty of the Lord: Praying with Icons* (Ave Maria Press, Inc., 1st rev. ed. 2007)

_____. *Reaching Out: The Three Movements of the Spiritual Life* (Doubleday Image Books, 1986)

O'Connor, Flannery. *The Complete Stories* (Farrar, Strauss & Giroux, 1971)

_____. *Mystery and Manners: Occasional Prose* (Farrar, Strauss & Giroux, 2000)

Pennock, Dee. *Who is God? Who Am I? Who Are You?* (St. Tikhon's Press, 1973)

Schmemann, Fr. Alexander. *For the Life of the World: Sacraments and Orthodoxy* (St. Vladimir's Seminary Press)

_____. *Of Water and the Spirit: A Liturgical Study of Baptism* (St. Vladimir's Seminary Press)

Vanier, Jean. *From Brokenness to Community* (Paulist Press, 1992)

Ware, Bp. Kallistos (Timothy). *The Orthodox Church* (Penguin Books, 1997)

SOME FAVORITE RECIPES

CELEBRATION FOOD FROM
THE COMMUNITY AT ST. JOHN'S

A TRADITIONAL EASTER BASKET

*Place the following items in a wicker basket and tie a ribbon bow to the
handle. A linen cover, usually embroidered with a picture of the risen Christ,
or with the words "Christ is Risen," is placed over the food when brought to
the church. At St. John's, our baskets are blessed at the end of the Paschal
Liturgy. The priest walks around the nave, sprinkling holy water on our
uplifted baskets, in preparation for special breakfasts in our homes.*

PASCHA BREAD—A sweet yeast bread, rich in eggs and butter, is symbolic of
Christ Himself, who is our true Bread. It is usually a round loaf, baked with a
golden crust, and decorated with a symbol indicative of Christ. Sometimes a
cross made of dough is placed on top, encircled by a braid, giving the loaf a
crowned effect. Also, the Greek abbreviation for the name of Christ—IC XC—
is frequently fashioned of dough and placed on top of the loaf.

CHEESE—A soft cheese is shaped into a ball and decorated, using cloves or
pepper balls, with a cross or the IC XC symbol of Christ. A bland cheese is
usually used, to remind us of the moderation that Christians should practice
in all things.

HAM—This meat is symbolic of the joy and abundance of Easter.

SAUSAGE—A spicy sausage indicates God's favor and generosity.

BACON—A piece of uncooked bacon, cured with spices, symbolizes God's mercy
to us.

EGGS—Hard-boiled and brightly decorated with Easter symbols, eggs represent new life and resurrection.

HORSERADISH—Horseradish, mixed with grated red beets, is symbolic of the Passion of Christ that is still in our minds, but sweetened with sugar to remind us of the joy of the Resurrection.

BUTTER—Butter, molded into the form of a lamb or small cross, reminds us of the goodness of Christ.

SALT—Salt is necessary for flavor and reminds the Christian of his duty to others.

DEBBIE'S PASCHA BREAD

The women of Christ the Savior Orthodox Church in North Royalton, Ohio (Debbie's family's first parish), got together to bake these loaves during Lent. After the Easter service, all the families gathered downstairs with their food-filled Easter baskets and loaves of Pascha bread, each with a lighted candle in the middle. The priest then blessed the baskets, and it was a sight to behold. Now, at Debbie's home on Easter morning, they also place a candle in their Pascha bread and sing the troparion together—Christ is risen from the dead!

6 T. warm water	2 eggs
½ pkg. yeast	6 T. sugar
¼ tsp. sugar	3½–4 c. flour
1 c. scalded milk	Grated peel of 1 lemon
2 T. butter	1 tsp. vanilla
2 T. oil	1 whole egg
¼ tsp. salt	1 T. water
1 c. flour	

Combine water, yeast, and ¼ tsp. sugar in a small bowl; let rest. In a large mixing bowl, pour scalded milk over butter, oil, and salt. Add 3 c. flour and combine with spoon. Let cool. Combine 2 eggs and 6 T. sugar in another bowl, beating them together. Add this, along with yeast mixture, to the large mixing bowl when flour and milk mixture is cool. Continue adding remaining flour, along with vanilla and lemon peel, using a wooden spoon, or hands, to combine. Do not use too much flour—dough should be slightly sticky.

Knead dough mixture about 20 minutes. Place in clean, oiled bowl, cover with a cloth, and let rise until doubled in size. (Debbie uses the top rack of a cool oven and place a bowl of boiling water on the lower rack.) Cut off small portion of dough to use for making decorations. Knead this small piece with a little flour and place in small bowl, cover with cloth, and set aside until later. Shape remaining dough into a round loaf and place into prepared round pan (lightly greased with butter). Let loaf rise again (use same method as above) for about 40 minutes, then remove from oven. Preheat oven to 375°.

Beat the whole egg and water together lightly, then brush it on top of loaf. Make decorations from the piece of reserved dough and place on top of loaf. (Debbie makes the Orthodox cross and the symbols of Jesus Christ—IC and XC.) Bake 15 minutes at 375°. Check after 10 minutes to prevent burning of top. Use foil to lightly cover exposed portions. Lower oven temperature to 325°. Brush top of loaf again with water/egg mixture and bake an additional 40–60 minutes at 325°.

When done, remove from oven, let cool 10 minutes in pan, then remove from pan and cool thoroughly on rack. (If baked in advance, store cooled loaves in ziplock bags and freeze until Holy Saturday.) Serve sliced with Pascha cheese spread.

PASCHA CHEESE SPREAD

4 (8 oz.) pkgs. cream cheese   3 egg yolks
1 c. butter   2 c. powdered sugar
2 tsp. vanilla

Allow cream cheese and butter to soften at room temperature. Combine all ingredients in a large mixing bowl to a thin consistency. Line round containers (I use

Rubbermaid ones) with a double layer of cheesecloth. Pour cheese mixture into containers and refrigerate, covered, until firm. Unmold when ready to eat. Decorate with raisins and/or almonds in form of cross with symbols IC/XC. Serve with Pascha bread. (Note: You may also add candied fruit and/or slivered almonds to cheese mixture.)

JUDI'S BAKLAVA

Who doesn't love this sweet favorite? Judi makes it every fall for the parish bazaar, and it also appears (but not for long) on the dessert table at special feasts and wedding receptions.

1 lb. fillo (phyllo) dough
1½ cups clarified butter ("sumnah"), melted [see next page]
Filling [see next page]
Syrup [see next page]

(Judi uses 1½ lb. fillo dough because she makes the baklava in a half-sheet cake pan. She advises that if the fillo sheets tear, they can still be used by patching them with other pieces. She puts a whole piece on the top and bottom.)

Sumnah (Clarified Butter):
2 lbs. butter

Place butter in a large saucepan over medium heat. The butter should come to a gentle boil. Let it continue boiling and stir it occasionally, allowing the salt to settle. The butter will appear clear at this point with some froth on top. The froth can be removed with a slotted spoon. (Clarifying butter takes time and care. Do not leave the butter unattended.)

When the butter is cool, drain carefully so that the salt remains on the bottom of the pan and only the clarified butter is poured into a container. Cover the butter. It does not need to be refrigerated: this allows the baklava to be kept at room temperature.

Note: Judi uses unsalted butter, which makes this process a little easier.

Filling:

2 lbs. ground walnuts or pecans (Judi prefers pecans; some people use pistachios)

½ c. sugar

1 tsp. nutmeg or ¼ tsp. cinnamon (Judi uses cinnamon)

Syrup:

2 c. sugar   1 c. water

1 T. lemon juice

To prepare the syrup, bring water, sugar, and lemon juice to a gentle boil. Simmer 5 minutes. Let syrup cool. Grind the nuts and season with sugar and nutmeg or cinnamon.

To assemble the baklava: Unfold the dough. Cut dough in half to create sheets the approximate size of the baking pan. Wrap half of dough in plastic to prevent drying. Working with remaining half, spread the pan and each leaf of dough with clarified butter. Layer dough in pan. Spread the filling evenly over the buttered dough. Top the filling with the remaining fillo dough, buttering each leaf. Cut the pastry into diamond shapes prior to baking. Bake at 325° F for 40–45 minutes or until golden. Remove from oven and pour cool syrup over the hot pastry.

Arrange baklava pieces in muffin papers or foil cups for serving.

Baking instructions for frozen baklava:

Baklava may be frozen before baking. Preheat oven to 200–225° (this temperature will make the pastry crisper). Remove tray from freezer. Do not allow the baklava to thaw or it will be soggy. Bake until golden (watch carefully; time may vary). Remove from oven and pour cool syrup over hot pastry.

BARBARA P.'S KOLIVA (MEMORIAL WHEAT)

There are many variations of this dish, according to individual and parish tastes. This recipe is just right for a Sunday Liturgy at St. John's. It makes two heaping punch bowls full.

15 c. raw wheat (hard)

6 c. currants

6 c. finely chopped nuts (your choice)

1–2 c. warm honey

Vanilla, cinnamon, or almond flavoring

1 pkg. graham crackers

Powdered sugar

Candied almonds or other decoration

Boil the wheat for 1–1½ hours. Drain and rinse with cold water. Drain dry. (Some spread it on a towel to dry.) Warm the honey, chop the nuts, and crush the graham crackers.

On the morning of the service, mix wheat, nuts, fruit, honey, and flavoring in a large pot. Spoon it into the punch bowls. Cover the top with graham cracker crumbs. Sift powdered sugar over the top. Decorate with chocolate-covered almonds, raisins, silver candies, or anything you like.

SHERRILYN'S MEMORIAL WHEAT

Sherrilyn's version is a bit sweeter than Barbara's. The one you prefer depends on your own or your parish's taste.

15 c. wheat berries

2 lb. walnuts, ground

2 lemons, juiced

1 lb. brown sugar

2 T. vanilla extract

1 box currants

1 box golden raisins

6 bags Nestle's chocolate raisins

    OR yogurt raisins

1 pkg. graham crackers, ground

powdered sugar, for sprinkling

Jordan almonds or candy, for decorating

Boil wheat 1½ hours. Drain, rinse, and drain dry. Grind walnuts, juice lemons, and grind graham crackers. Keep cracker crumbs separate until the last step.

On the morning of the service, mix wheat, nuts, dried fruit, brown sugar, flavorings, and lemon juice in a large bowl. Spoon mixture into punch bowls. Cover tops with ground graham crackers. (This keeps the powdered sugar from melting away.) Sift powdered sugar over the top. Decorate with candy and Jordan almonds in the shape of a cross. Makes two full punch bowls.

ROSALIE'S SHRIMP SALAD

Rosalie started a now-cherished tradition among several families of gathering for a seafood supper following the liturgies of Christmas Eve and Holy Saturday. The menu always includes a big dish of shrimp salad. Over the years, I have adapted this recipe to include flaked crab and a generous shake of Old Bay seafood seasoning.

1 pkg. small shell pasta	½ c. mayonnaise
1 lb. frozen shrimp meat or salad shrimp	1 tsp. seasoned salt
8 oz. flaked crab meat	1 tsp. dill weed
½ c. celery, chopped	¼ tsp. pepper
½ c. onion (white or green), chopped	Old Bay seasoning, to taste

Cook pasta according to package directions. Drain pasta and place in a serving bowl. Add shrimp. Combine remaining ingredients and mix thoroughly with pasta and shrimp. Chill 1 hour before serving.

COOK FAMILY'S CHRISTMAS MONKEY BREAD

These are perfect to serve to your family and friends on Christmas morning, as they can be made early and left to rise during Christmas liturgy. We always come home from church, start the coffee, and bake the Monkey Bread, then snack on it while we exchange presents.

¾ c. pecans, coarsely chopped

1 box butterscotch pudding (not instant)

6 T. melted butter

18 frozen uncooked yeast rolls

¾ c. brown sugar

¼ tsp. cinnamon

Spray Bundt pan or angel food cake pan with nonstick spray. Sprinkle pecan pieces on bottom of pan and arrange frozen rolls on top of pecans. Drizzle half of melted butter or margarine on top of rolls. Combine sugar and cinnamon. Sprinkle half of this over rolls. Sprinkle pudding mix on rolls, followed by remaining sugar/cinnamon mixture and melted butter. Cover with towel and let rise. Bake at 350° for 30 minutes. Invert onto serving plate immediately. Pull apart and enjoy!

LORI'S MOOSE BARLEY STEW

Lori often makes this stew and takes it on camping trips, including the annual summer gathering at the Kasilof River. The recipe always seems to make more than enough to feed everyone in camp and any others who may stop by to join us.

2 lb. moose steak or roast, cubed

2 T. oil

1 lg. onion, chopped

1½ tsp. salt

2 tsp. Worcestershire sauce

1 stalk celery, chopped

2 c. carrots, sliced

1–2 tsp. dried parsley

10–12 c. water

2 T. beef bouillon or 3 bouillon cubes

1 tsp. dried basil, crushed

1 c. pearl barley

salt & pepper, to taste

In a large kettle or Dutch oven, brown moose meat in hot oil over low heat. Stir in water, onion, bouillon, salt, basil, and Worcestershire sauce. Cover and simmer for 1 hour. Stir in carrots, celery, barley, and parsley. Cover and simmer for 45 minutes longer, or until barley is soft. Season with salt and pepper and serve.

BIG HOUSE CARDAMOM BRAID

This fragrant bread is perfect for any celebration. The basic recipe first appeared in a 1988 cookbook written by the "St. John's Antiochian Women," and was included in a section of recipes associated with the Big House. Cardamom Braid is baked for our Christmas Eve and Holy Saturday suppers by Rosalie's daughters—Mary Ruth, Rebecca, and Martha—and by Maye, the friend who first invited Rosalie to visit the community.

1 pkg. active dry yeast	1 egg
¾ c. milk	½ tsp. salt
¼ c. margarine	¾ tsp. ground cardamom
⅓ c. sugar	2¾–3 c. flour

Dissolve yeast in ½ c. warm milk. Cream the margarine and sugar. Beat in the egg. Add yeast mixture, remaining milk, salt, and cardamom. Add flour to make a soft dough. Knead until smooth and elastic. Place in greased bowl and let rise until double. Divide in thirds. Roll into long ropes. Braid together. Let rise until double. Bake at 375° for 30 minutes.

FATHER MARC AND KH. BETSY'S GRILLED SALMON

We at St. John's like to serve grilled salmon at summer feasts, including Transfiguration in early August. Salmon is especially tasty if it has just been caught or dipped from our favorite spots on the Kasilof and Kenai Rivers. This recipe came to the Dunaway family from a dear friend, Fr. Simeon Berven of blessed memory. Adjust the ingredient amounts if grilling for a crowd.

2 Alaskan salmon fillets	½ c. butter or margarine
1 onion, chopped	½ c. lemon juice

In a saucepan, cook butter, onion, and lemon juice until onion is tender. Remove from heat and set aside. Place aluminum foil over the rack of your grill (can use gas or charcoal grill, or wood fire). Lay the salmon fillets on the foil, skin side down. It is helpful to keep the fillets close together and to put the thicker sides toward the center, where there is more heat. Spoon butter mixture liberally over each fillet. Cook on medium-high heat for 10 minutes with lid closed. Check thick part of fillet with a fork. Salmon is done when it flakes with a fork and is no longer wet-looking. To serve, slide spatula just under meat; skin will stick to foil, which is discarded for easy cleanup.

LORI'S PSARI PLAKI

This dish is served at the St. John's traditional Annunciation dinner (fish, wine, and oil are allowed on Annunciation although it generally falls during Lent). It can be prepared the day before and refrigerated. The recipe is portioned for six servings, but it can be adjusted to serve as many as needed. (For the St. John's feast, Lori increases the recipe by twenty times.) Serve basmati rice with peas and carrots, rolls, green salad, and wine with Psari Plaki.

1½ lbs. fish fillets (salmon or halibut), cut into serving pieces
1 c. canned, or 3 diced, fresh tomatoes
1 bunch celery, chopped
2 small onions, chopped
1 clove garlic, minced
½ c. white wine
6 slices lemon

¼ c. lemon juice
⅓ c. olive oil
½ c. fresh parsley, chopped
OR 3 tsp. dried parsley
½ c. bread crumbs OR croutons
Crushed oregano
Salt & pepper, to taste

Arrange fillets in a single layer in a greased casserole dish. Season with salt, pepper, and oregano. In a large pot, make sauce by combining tomatoes, celery, onions, garlic, olive oil, lemon juice, and wine. Bring to boil and simmer until vegetables are tender, but firm. Pour sauce over fish fillets. Sprinkle with parsley and crumbs or croutons. Place a lemon slice on top of each serving and bake at 350° for 30–40 minutes, or until fish flakes when tested. (Note: If making ahead of time, leave crumbs or croutons off until ready to bake.)

PHEBE'S SMOKED SALMON SPREAD

You can make this delicious spread anytime, even if you don't have any smoked salmon in your pantry or freezer, with a handy bottle of Liquid Smoke. If you are lucky enough to have salmon fillets in your freezer, you can substitute a couple of them (cooked, of course) for the canned salmon.

1 (15½ oz.) can salmon	3 drops Tabasco sauce
(or 2 7¾ oz. cans)	3 T. parsley, minced
1 (8 oz.) pkg. cream cheese, softened	1 tsp. onion, grated
2 tsp. prepared horseradish	1 T. lemon juice
¼ tsp. Liquid Smoke	⅓ c. pecans, chopped
⅛ tsp. salt	

Drain and flake salmon. In a bowl, combine cream cheese, salmon, onion, horse-radish, lemon juice, liquid smoke, salt, and Tabasco sauce. Blend together thoroughly. Chill several hours. Combine pecans and parsley. Shape salmon mixture into a ball or fish shape. Roll in nut mixture. Chill. Serve as a spread with crisp crackers.

ABOUT THE AUTHOR

Mary Alice Cook, the daughter of a foundry worker and a secretary, grew up in a small industrial town in East Texas. As a child, her favorite pastimes were reading and writing unfinished stories and books; her family's life revolved around the little Southern Baptist church where she was baptized at age 9. In 1976, just after their marriage, she and her husband Bill drove north to a new home in Anchorage, Alaska. Their three sons were born and raised in Alaska, and the whole family was chrismated into the Orthodox  Church on February 2, 1992. A year later, they decided to make their home near St. John's Cathedral in Eagle River. Mary Alice earned a degree from the University of Alaska, Anchorage, but wife and mother was her main occupation until she recently returned to school to study for a graduate degree in Public History, with an emphasis on museum and archival work. She continues to write, both fiction and nonfiction, on a variety of topics.